750

Nutritious and Delicious

Lifetime Weight Management Basics
Educational Manual
Instructor Manual

What To Do About What You Weigh
Participant Manual
Trainer Manual

Nutritious and Delicious II

Becky Plumlee, M. Ed.

Nutritious and Delicious II

Recipe Illustrations by
Mandy Plumlee

Library of Congress Catalog No. TX–3–440–268
ISBN 0–9637340–9–1

For information please contact:
Becky Plumlee
705 North State Street, #102
Bellingham, WA 98225
(206) 734-4856

Recipe Illustrations: Mandy Plumlee
Cover (Flower)Watercolor Illustration: Maureen Braun, RN
Cover and Book Design & Illustration: Scott Montgomery
Printer: Northwest Graphics, Mount Vernon, WA

For all those who enjoyed and supported
my first cookbook, *Nutritious and Delicious,*
and
dedicated
to the memory of
my Aunt Tot.

A Note
from the Author

The information provided by nutritional analyses of recipes is extremely important. Although, most restaurants and grocery stores do NOT divulge this data about their prepared foods, it is readily available in most periodicals and cookbooks published today. Indeed, all health conscious consumers should be demanding this information. This is not happening largely because many consumers do not know how to interpret the numbers and then use the information to make wise food purchase and preparation decisions. FOR EXAMPLE: most individuals still think *kcalories per serving* is the most important nutritional number. Even if you understand that the *fat data* is what you need to look for, the *number of fat grams per serving* can only have meaning when you understand how many fat grams are appropriate per day.

The following nutritional guidelines should provide you with a better understanding of the importance of knowing what is in foods and why it is crucial to insist on complete nutritional information about all food products. This includes foods served in restaurants and grocery stores and ALL RECIPES published in magazines, newspapers, and cookbooks.

1. No more than 20% of total kcaloric intake per day should be FAT.

2. Not more than 10% of total kcaloric intake should be refined sugar.

3. Total dietary cholesterol consumption per day should not exceed 200mg.

4. Sodium intake should not be more that 2200 – 2400 mg. per day.

5. The average person should not consume more than 44 GRAMS OF FAT PER DAY.

6. Not more than 10% of total daily food intake should be SATURATED FAT.

7. Focus on reducing TOTAL FAT INTAKE in order to lower blood cholesterol level.

8. 65% to 68% of our food intake should be complex carbohydrates (whole grain breads, rice, pasta, potatoes, cereals, legumes, fruits, and vegetables).

9. Consumption of dietary fiber should be at least 35 grams per day.

10. The single most important thing you can do today to improve your health and maintain a normal bodyfat level over your lifetime is to begin EXERCISING aerobically a minimum of 4 to 5 times per week.

CONTENTS

DESSERTS

SNACKS, SAUCES & SIDE DISHES

Introduction

This cookbook, like the first *Nutritious and Delicious*, has an educational purpose. While the first book introduced the basic methods of lowfat, low-salt, low-sugar cooking, *Nutritious and Delicious II* has been designed to teach basic recipe alteration techniques, simply and effectively.

Along with the public's growing awareness of the need to meet healthier nutritional guidelines, many new food products have been introduced that can be helpful in the reduction of dietary fat and sodium. This cookbook can be an informative and time-saving aid to those desiring to modify their favorite not-so-healthy recipes. It teaches basic ingredient substitution methods and demonstrates appropriate usage of the latest lowfat and nonfat products. Again, in keeping with the author's belief that most cooks have limited time in the kitchen, the recipes are simple, quick to prepare, rely on basic ingredients, and are generally appealing to adults and children alike.

All of the original recipes in this cookbook have been altered to help individuals meet the new dietary composition guidelines: 12 - 15 % protein; 65 - 68 % carbohydrate; 20 % fat. THIS IS *NOT* A "DIET" COOKBOOK! It is a cookbook with delicious recipes for those who are ready to make the food selection changes necessary for good health, based on what we know today.

A special thank-you to all of the individuals who contributed recipes that needed altering: former *Lifetime Weight Management Basics* group participants, private clients, friends, and family. You have all helped make this book possible. Finally, I will be forever grateful to my good friend and proofreader, Donna Dutton.

Recipe
Alteration Technique
Basics

—

•

Introduction

•

Ten Basic Recipe Alteration Guidelines

•

Flavor without much Fat, Sodium, or Sugar

INTRODUCTION

Most people feel very uncomfortable altering ingredient amounts listed in a written recipe or making product substitutions when cooking. This is, of course, very understandable. The thought of spending an hour or more preparing a meal that turns out to be unsatisfactory is reason enough to be hesitant.

Unfortunately, many recipes do not meet the new healthy eating guidelines in terms of sodium, fat and sugar content. Some of the recipes and cooking techniques we learned from our parents have turned out to be hazardous to health. Consequently, if we want to keep eating our favorite foods, we need to learn how to prepare them in a healthier fashion. The good news is, this is not difficult or time consuming.

First, you will need to become familiar with the abundant food products now available to help you prepare your daily meals according to the new nutritional guidelines. Spend some extra time in your local supermarket locating the products listed below:

lowfat / nonfat cheeses
egg substitute
diet margarine
nonfat / lowfat milk, yogurt, cottage cheese
salt-free canned tomatoes and tomato sauce
reduced-sugar syrup and jam
powdered buttermilk
evaporated skim milk
lite cake mixes
extra lean ground turkey and beef
lowfat / nonfat frozen dairy desserts
whole grain flours
low-salt soups and broth
low-salt and butter flavored seasonings
low-sugar / low-salt cereals and nonfat granola
non-stick cooking and baking equipment

Ten
Basic Recipe Alteration
Guidelines

Altering recipes is really quite simple. Follow the TEN BASIC common-sense guidelines:

1. The amount of sugar in a standard recipe can be reduced by at least half without affecting the taste or texture significantly.

2. When reducing oil in a recipe, replace it with an equal amount of some other liquid.

3. Shortening can be replaced with diet margarine in most recipes (use brands with 6 grams of fat per tablespoon). Begin using reduced-fat margarine in all cooking and baking.

4. In all baked goods, replace half of refined white flour with whole wheat flour (purchase in bulk section of supermarket) for added nutritional value and texture.

5. Choose muffin and dessert recipes that contain fruit or fruit juice; these recipes retain moisture and flavor when fat is reduced.

6. Begin selecting lowfat dairy products and move to the nonfat products as soon as possible, especially for cooking purposes.

7. Reduce or omit salt in all cooking and baking.

8. Reduce fat and cholesterol by substituting each whole egg with two egg whites or ¼ cup egg substitute (that's right, just throw the yolks away!).

9. With the exception of light stir-frying, frying is one cooking technique that should be discontinued.

10. Begin using meat, fish and poultry as a condiment in your meals rather than the main attraction. Think COMPLEX CARBOHYDRATES!

Flavor without much Fat, Sodium, or Sugar

As a population, Americans are typically very accustomed to a high level of sodium, sugar and fat in their foods. This is largely the result of relying on prepackaged, processed foods. Food manufacturers can keep their prices lower by using the cheapest spices available; salt and sugar. In addition, it is much cheaper and easier to use fat for moisture and flavor.

In order to reduce the three main additives in our diets, some re-education in the use of other spices and flavorings will be required; otherwise foods with a reduced fat, sodium and sugar content will taste like cardboard and developing new taste preferences will be difficult. Begin learning about spices and flavorings by choosing recipes that contain them; such as, Italian and Mexican dishes. It is easy to remove fat and yet retain flavor in recipes that contain the following spices, herbs and flavorings:

Spices	Herbs	Flavorings
allspice	basil	vanilla extract
cardamom	bay leaf	almond extract
cinnamon	caraway seed	orange/orange peel
cloves	dill	lemon/lemon peel
ginger	marjoram	butter flavoring
nutmeg	dry mustard	anise seed/extract
mace	oregano	rum flavoring
chili powder	tarragon	brandy flavoring
curry powder	thyme	coconut flavoring
cumin	rosemary	walnut flavoring

*Also, utilize *Mrs. Dash's* salt free spice combinations and mixed Italian spices.

Main Dishes

—

•

Basic Recipe Alteration Techniques

•

Main Dishes

1. Reduce the amount of meat and poultry included in all main dishes (1–2 cups is plenty for four servings). Remember that only one 3–5 oz. serving of lean meat, fish or poultry per day is optimal for good health (3 oz. for women; 4–5 oz. for men and growing teenagers).

2. Prepare meat and poultry in the slow cooker or by broiling, baking, microwaving, or roasting. Never add fat and remove all skin and visible fat before cooking.

3. Little or no fat is necessary when using non-stick pans. Sauteing in broth or wine is a totally fat-free option.

4. Substitute evaporated skim milk in all recipes calling for cream. Substitute nonfat or lowfat yogurt for sour cream, and skim or lowfat milk for whole milk. Buttermilk is also fat free and can be purchased in powdered form.

5. Use cornstarch as a thickening agent. It does not require any fat.

6. Use *Butter Buds* or *Molly McButter* if you want vegetables to taste buttery.

The above alteration techniques and many more will be demonstrated and explained in the recipe examples to follow. Remember that your goal should be to retain the flavor and texture of the original recipe as much as possible when altering it to reduce sodium, sugar, and fat.

If you are just beginning to modify your dietary intake, it is important to be conservative in your recipe ingredient reductions and substitutions. You can always reduce fat, sugar, and salt more severely after your taste buds have begun to adjust to the initial changes. The first recipe alteration example shows how to institute gradual changes in taste preferences.

Example #1 – Main Dishes

CREAMY MUSHROOMS AND PASTA

Original Recipe:	Alterations #1:	Alterations #2:
1 lb. fresh mushrooms		
4 Tbls. butter	**4 Tbls. margarine*	**4 Tbls. diet margarine*
½ cup minced onion		
8 oz. egg noodles	**8 oz. non-egg pasta*	
1 cup sour cream	**1 cup lite sour cream*	**1 cup regular, lowfat or nonfat yogurt*
¼ cup chopped parsley		
1 ½ tsps. salt	**Omit*	
¼ tsp. pepper		
1 cup soft bread crumbs	**1 cup soft whole wheat bread crumbs*	

Directions

RINSE and slice mushrooms. Melt 3 Tbls. diet margarine in a non-stick skillet and saute the mushrooms and onions until tender, about 5 minutes. Combine the cooked pasta, mushrooms, lowfat yogurt, parsley, and pepper. Spoon into a 2 quart sprayed casserole dish.

MELT remaining margarine in the skillet and add the bread crumbs, tossing lightly. Spoon around the edge of the casserole dish. Bake at 400 for about 5 - 10 minutes until hot. Makes 6 servings.

Nutritional Analysis:	Original	#1	#2	#3	
			(reg.)	(low / nonfat)	
Kcals. =	381	349	286	286	284
Chol. =	39 mg	16 mg	6 mg	3 mg	1.5 mg
Sodium =	759 mg	245 mg	249 mg	258 mg	260 mg
Fat =	18 grams	14 grams	7 g	6 g	5.5 g
Fat % =	41 %	35 %	21 %	19 %	17 %

Illustrated Alteration Technique Example #1:

1. Use diet margarine (6 grams of fat per tablespoon) in place of regular margarine.

2. Use non-egg pastas to reduce cholesterol.

3. Substitute lowfat yogurt for sour cream.

4. Use whole grain bread or bread crumbs.

5. Make substitutions and alterations gradually.

Example #2 - Main Dishes

SOUR CREAM SUPREME

Original Recipe:

1 ½ lb. ground beef
1 clove minced garlic
2 (8 oz.) cans tomato sauce
1 tsp. salt and pepper
12 oz. noodles
1 Tbls. brown sugar
6 oz. cream cheese
1 cup sour cream
1 chopped onion
½ lb. grated cheddar cheese

Alterations:

*8 oz. lean ground turkey

*24 oz. low-salt tomato sauce
*Omit salt
*16 oz. non-egg pasta
*1 – 2 Tbls. wine
*6 oz. nonfat cream cheese
*8 oz. nonfat yogurt

*2 oz. shredded fresh Parmesan cheese
*1 tsp. each oregano, basil, marjoram

Directions:

SAUTE ground turkey, onion and garlic in a non-stick pan. Add the tomato sauce, pepper, wine, and spices; simmer about 20 minutes. Blend the yogurt and cream cheese until smooth. Cook the pasta according to package directions.

LAYER half the meat sauce, cheese mixture, and pasta in a 9X13 non-stick pan; repeat with a second layer of each and top with the shredded Parmesan cheese. Bake at 350 for 25 to 30 minutes. Makes 6 servings (serve with colorful salad and Italian bread).

Nutritional Analysis:	Original	Lowfat Version
Kcals. =	895	491
Chol. =	186 mg	34 mg
Sodium =	1244 mg	266 mg
Fat =	53 grams	9 grams
Fat % =	53 %	17 %

Illustrated Alteration Technique Example #2:

1. Substitute lean ground turkey for ground beef.
2. Reduce total amount of meat.
3. Use low-sodium tomato products.
4. Omit added salt when cooking. Add a little at the table if necessary.
5. Use lowfat or nonfat dairy products.
6. Substitute Parmesan cheese for other high fat cheese when appropriate.
7. Use herbs and spices in recipes that have relied on fat and salt for flavor.

CHICKEN WITH ORANGE SAUCE

Original Recipe:

1 broiler/fryer coated with
* seasoned flour*
¼ cup butter
½ cup orange juice
1 tsp. Worcestershire sauce

Alterations:

*Use 6 skinned chicken breasts seasoned
* with* Mrs. Dash's *spicy seasoning*
*Omit
*Plus ½ Tbls. cornstarch
*Use low-sodium Worcestershire

Directions:

PLACE seasoned chicken breasts in a non-stick baking pan. Thicken the orange juice by combining with the cornstarch and stirring over medium heat. Add the Worcestershire sauce to the hot orange sauce. Evenly spread the sauce over the chicken pieces. Bake, lightly covered, at 400 for about 30 minutes. Uncover and continue baking for another 10 minutes. Serve with a rice pilaf and cooked fresh asparagus or broccoli.

Makes 6 servings.

Nutritional Analysis:

	Original	Lowfat Version
Kcals. =	367	140
Chol. =	118 mg	68 mg
Sodium =	216 mg	133 mg
Fat =	24 grams	1 gram
Fat % =	59 %	10 %

SPICY PEANUT CHICKEN

Original Recipe:

1 cup sliced onion
12 oz. skinless, boneless chicken breasts
1 tsp. cumin
1/2 tsp. ground cinnamon
1 - 2 Tbls. canola oil
2 plum tomatoes
1/2 jalapeno pepper
1 Tbls. lemon juice
2 Tbls. peanut butter
1/2 tsp. minced garlic
1/2 cup no-salt tomato sauce
Garnish with fresh cilantro

Alterations:

*Omit oil; use 2 Tbls. white wine

Directions:

WASH AND DRY chicken breasts and rub with cumin and cinnamon on both sides. In a large non-stick skillet or sauce pan, saute the onion and chicken. Cut plum tomatoes in chunks and puree in food processor along with the jalapeno pepper, lemon juice, peanut butter, garlic, and tomato sauce. Pour sauce over chicken and cover. Reduce heat and simmer about 10 minutes or until chicken is cooked. Serve sauce with chicken over rice and garnish with cilantro. Makes 6 servings.

Nutritional Analysis:	Original	Lowfat Version
Kcals. =	278	222
Chol. =	65 mg	65 mg
Sodium =	105 mg	105 mg
Fat =	14 grams	7 grams
Fat % =	44 %	29 %

EASY CHICKEN BREASTS IN WINE SAUCE

Original Recipe:

1 cup raw rice

6 skinned chicken breasts
8 oz. drained, canned mushrooms
1 can cream of mushroom soup
1 soup can of water
1 package onion soup mix

½ cup white wine

Alterations:

*Use a mixture of brown/white and wild rice

*2 cups fresh sliced mushrooms
*Use Campbell's Healthy Request

*2 Tbls. dried onion flakes + Mrs. Dash's *seasoning* + 2 low-sodium beef broth packets

Directions:

USE A NON-STICK 9X13 casserole dish or coat with vegetable spray. Place rice evenly over the bottom and then chicken on top of rice. Combine mushrooms, soup, broth, chopped onion, seasonings, and wine until thoroughly blended. Pour over chicken. Seal with foil and bake at 350 for 1 ½ hours. Serves 6. This recipe can be made up in advance or cooked in a slow cooker on low all day.

Nutritional Analysis:	Original	Low Sodium Version
Kcals. =	333	302
Chol. =	69 mg	69 mg
Sodium =	1160 mg	305 mg
Fat =	6 grams	4 grams
Fat % =	18 %	13 %

QUICK CHICKEN RICE CASSEROLE

Original Recipe:
6 uncooked chicken breasts
1 ½ cups raw rice
3 cans mushroom soup
3 soup cans of milk
1 package onion soup mix

Alterations:
*6 skinned chicken breasts
*Use at least half brown rice
*Use Campbell's Healthy Request
*Use nonfat milk
*4 packages low-sodium beef broth + 2
   Tbls. dehydrated onions + 1 Tbls.
   Mrs. Dash's *no-salt spices*

Directions:

PLACE rice evenly over the bottom of a non-stick 9X13 pan, or coat pan with cooking spray before adding rice. Top rice with the skinned chicken breasts. Combine the soup with milk, stirring until smooth and creamy. Add the onions, spices, and broth mix to the soup. Pour over chicken and bake COVERED at 350 for about 1 ½ hours. Hot cooked vegetables and a fruit/whole grain type dessert completes this meal. Serves 6.

Nutritional Analysis:

	Original	Lowfat Version
Kcals. =	686	463
Chol. =	114 mg	72 mg
Sodium =	1900 mg	809 mg
Fat =	32 grams	9 grams
Fat % =	42 %	18 %

CHICKEN DIVAN

Original Recipe:

*3 boned whole chicken breasts (18 oz.)
cooked and cubed*
10 oz. broccoli, thawed
1 can cream of chicken soup

⅓ cup mayonnaise
½ tsp. lemon juice
½ tsp. curry powder
1 cup grated cheddar cheese

Alterations:

*12 oz. boned chicken breasts

*16 - 20 oz. broccoli, thawed
** ½ can Healthy Request + 10 oz.
evaporated skim milk*
* ⅓ cup nonfat mayonnaise
*1 tsp. lemon juice
*1 tsp. curry powder
*1 cup grated lowfat cheddar cheese
*1 cup brown rice, cooked

Directions:

PLACE the broccoli in the bottom of a sprayed or non-stick casserole dish; top with cubed chicken. Combine the soup, milk, mayonnaise, lemon juice, and curry powder. Pour sauce over the broccoli and chicken. Sprinkle with grated cheese and bake at 350 for 35 minutes. Serve over the cooked brown rice. Makes 4 servings.

Nutritional Analysis:

Nutritional Analysis:	Original	Lowfat Version
Kcals. =	556	543
Chol. =	154 mg	98 mg
Sodium =	994 mg	634 mg
Fat =	34 grams	14 grams
Fat % =	56 %	24 %

PARMESAN DIJON CHICKEN

Original Recipe:

3 slices white bread
1 cup Parmesan cheese, grated
⅓ cup melted margarine
⅔ cup Dijon mustard
3 Tbls. white wine
24 oz. boneless, skinless, chicken breasts

Alterations:

*3 slices whole wheat bread
* ½ cup Parmesan cheese, grated
* ⅓ cup prepared Butter Buds
* ⅓ - ½ cup Dijon mustard
*4 - 5 Tbls. wine or apple juice

Directions:

IN FOOD PROCESSOR, make bread crumbs out of sliced bread. Combine crumbs with the Parmesan cheese. Mix the mustard with the wine or juice. Dip chicken pieces in wine mixture and roll in the bread crumbs. Place in a non-stick casserole and drizzle with *Butter Buds*. Bake at about 500 for 15 - 20 minutes. 8 servings.

Nutritional Analysis:

	Original	Lowfat Version
Kcals. =	307	214
Chol. =	80 mg	76 mg
Sodium =	668 mg	458 mg
Fat =	16 grams	7 grams
Fat % =	47 %	29 %

HAWAIIAN CHICKEN

Original Recipe:

Use legs, breasts, & thighs of two
    fryer chickens
½ cup flour
⅓ cup salad oil
¼ tsp. pepper
20 oz. sliced pineapple, reserve juice
2 cups white sugar
4 Tbls. cornstarch
1 ½ cups cider vinegar

2 Tbls. soy sauce
½ tsp. dry ginger
2 chicken bouillon cubes

Alterations:

*24 oz. skinned, boned, chicken breasts

*Omit
*Omit

*5 Tbls. sugar

* ½ cup cider vinegar + 2 ½ cups
    pineapple juice
*2 Tbls. low-sodium soy sauce
*1 tsp. ginger
*3 packets low-sodium chicken broth
*1 cup green pepper slices
*1 cup cooked carrots
*8 oz. drained water chestnuts
*8 cups cooked brown rice

Directions:

COOK the chicken breasts in the microwave or on top of the stove with a small amount of water until tender; cool and cut into cubes. Pre-cook the carrots and peppers in the microwave, also.

MIX the remaining sauce ingredients: sliced pineapple, pineapple juice, vinegar, cornstarch, soy sauce, ginger, bouillon, pepper, and sugar. Cook over medium heat, stirring frequently, until thickened. Add the chicken, cooked vegetables, and water chestnuts; simmer on low. Serve over hot cooked brown rice. Makes 8 servings.

Nutritional Analysis:

	Original	Lowfat Version
Kcals. =	830	516
Chol. =	94 mg	72 mg
Sodium =	866 mg	351 mg
Fat =	23 grams	6 grams
Fat % =	24 %	10 %

CHICKEN ROLLS
WITH PASTA

Original Recipe:

4 large chicken breasts (halved, skinned
    and boned) about 12 oz.
4 slices Monterey Jack cheese (1 oz.)
4 Tbls. dry bread crumbs
8 tsp. grated Parmesan cheese

1 Tbls. dried parsley
4 Tbls. melted butter
3 cups cooked noodles
2 cups frozen broccoli cuts
1 ⅓ cups pizza or spaghetti sauce

Alterations:

*Or use turkey breast cutlets

*4 slices lowfat Monterey Jack cheese
*1 ½ cups dry bread crumbs
*Use 1 Tbl. Mrs. Dash's salt-free
    seasonings instead of Parmesan

*4 Tbls. barbecue sauce + 4 Tbls. water
*6 cups cooked pasta
*3 cups frozen broccoli cuts
*2 cups no-salt tomato sauce seasoned
    with Italian spices

Directions:

WITH A MEAT MALLET, pound the chicken breasts (between two sheets of waxed paper) to ¼ inch thickness. Place cheese slices on chicken breasts, cutting to fit within ¼ inch of edges. Fold in sides; roll up jelly-roll fashion, pressing to seal. In a cereal bowl combine the bread crumbs, the *Mrs. Dash's* seasonings, and parsley. Dip chicken rolls in the barbecue sauce mixed with water and then roll in crumbs. Place in a non-stick casserole and bake, covered, for about 20 minutes at 500. Uncover and bake about 10 minutes longer until crisp but tender and juicy.

WHILE chicken is baking, cook frozen broccoli in microwave seasoning with some *Mrs. Dash's* spices and *Molly McButter*, if desired (about 8 minutes cooking time). In a non-stick sauce pan, heat cooked pasta with the spiced tomato sauce; keep pasta and vegetables warm until chicken is cooked. Serve at once. 4 servings.

Nutritional Analysis:

	Original	Lowfat Version
Kcals. =	670	733
Chol. =	168 mg	89 mg
Sodium =	865 mg	963 mg
Carbs =	53 grams	92 grams
Fat =	31 grams	17 grams
Fat % =	42 %	21 %

HOT CHICKEN SALAD

Original Recipe:

3 cups cubed cooked chicken or turkey
2 cups sliced celery
½ red pepper, chopped
2 cups toasted whole wheat bread cubes
½ cup golden raisins
½ cup lite sour cream or regular yogurt or lite mayonnaise
¾ cup nonfat yogurt
½ cup grated lowfat Jack cheese
¼ cup grated Parmesan cheese
4 baked potatoes

Directions:

MIX all ingredients except potatoes together lightly. Put in a non-stick baking dish (9X13) and top with ½ cup of grated lowfat Jack cheese and sprinkle with ¼ cup Parmesan cheese. Bake for 30 minutes at 350. Serve with a salad and a baked potato. 4 servings.

Nutritional Analysis: (includes baked potato)

Kcals. =	640
Chol. =	93 mg
Sodium =	528 mg
Fat =	12 grams
Fat % =	17 %

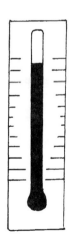

COQ AU VIN

Original Recipe:

5 bacon slices, cooked
⅔ cup sliced green onion
2 ½ lbs. chicken breasts
4 - 6 small white onions
¼ lb. whole mushrooms
6 - 8 small new potatoes
1 clove garlic, minced
Salt and pepper to taste
1 tsp. thyme
½ cup chicken broth
½ cup Burgundy wine
1 Tbls. dried parsley

Alterations:

*1 slice Canadian Bacon, diced

*Remove skin

*Omit salt

*Use low-sodium brand

Directions:

PUT all ingredients in the crock-pot and cook on low 8 - 10 hours. Serves 6.

Nutritional Analysis:

	Original	Lowfat Version
Kcals. =	424	278
Chol. =	124 mg	111 mg
Sodium =	546 mg	284 mg
Fat =	20 grams	3 grams
Fat % =	46 %	9 %

TUNA OR CHICKEN SOUFFLE CASSEROLE

Original Recipe:

12 slices of bread, buttered

2 cans water packed tuna, drained
1 cup diced celery
1 Tbls. diced onion
1 cup mayonnaise
¼ cup milk
1 can mushrooms, drained
4 eggs
2 cups milk
1 can mushroom soup

Alterations:

**12 slices whole grain bread; spread
  lightly with diet margarine*
*Or use 12 oz. cooked chicken breast

*Increase to ½ cup
*Use nonfat mayonnaise
* ¼ cup nonfat milk
*1 cup fresh mushrooms
*1 cup Egg Beaters
*2 cups nonfat milk
*Use Healthy Request

Directions:

LINE the bottom of a non-stick baking dish with 6 slices of whole grain bread (spread both sides with diet margarine; about 1 tsp. per side). Cover bread with chicken or tuna, diced celery, and diced onion. Mix the mayonnaise, ¼ cup milk, and the mushrooms; pour over bread and chicken. Place the remaining coated bread slices over the previous layers. Beat the *Egg Beaters* with the 2 cups of nonfat milk and pour over all. Let stand overnight. Just before baking, spread casserole with the mushroom soup. Bake about 1 hour at 350. Serves 8. Add a tossed green salad and fresh melon for a complete meal.

Nutritional Analysis:

	Original	Lowfat Version
Kcals. =	583	300
Chol. =	189 mg	28 mg
Sodium =	919 mg	680 mg
Fat =	42 grams	9 grams
Fat % =	65 %	27 %

ZIPPY SAUSAGE STRATA

Original Recipe:

2 lbs. pork sausage, cooked & drained
1 lb. shredded Monterey Jack cheese
1 lb. shredded cheddar cheese
8 slices bread, buttered
8 eggs, slightly beaten
2 ½ cups milk

1 tsp. salt
½ tsp. pepper
¼ tsp. dry mustard
Dash of garlic powder
4 oz. diced green chili
8 Tbls. salsa

Alterations:

*8 oz. spiced ground turkey, cooked
*4 oz. shredded lowfat Jack cheese
*4 oz. shredded lowfat cheddar cheese
*10 slices cracked wheat bread
*2 cups Egg Beaters
*1 cup evaporated skimmed + 1 ½ cups
   nonfat milk
*Omit

* ½ tsp. dry mustard
* ¼ tsp. garlic powder

*Plus ½ cup chopped green onion

Directions:

SAUTE the turkey sausage and green onion; set aside. Combine the shredded cheeses. In a 9X13 non-stick pan, cover bottom with 5 slices of the bread; cover with half the sausage and half the cheese. Repeat layering. Combine the *Egg Beaters*, milk, pepper, mustard, and garlic powder. Pour egg mixture over layers. Top all with the chopped chilies. Cover and put in refrigerator overnight. Can be stored up to 3 days. Bake at 325 for 1 ½ hours. Serve with salsa. 8 servings.

Nutritional Analysis:

	Original	Lowfat Version
Kcals. =	920	292
Chol. =	333 mg	35 mg
Sodium =	1748 mg	681 mg
Fat =	74 grams	11 grams
Fat % =	73 %	32 %

STIR FRIED RICE AND VEGETABLES

Original Recipe:	Alterations:
2 cups raw long grain rice	**1 cup each, long grain and wild rice*
2 cups chicken broth	**Use low-sodium*
2 cups water	
2 Tbls. Worcestershire sauce	**Use low-sodium*
1 Tbls. margarine	**Use diet margarine*
2 tsp. salt	**Omit*
2 cloves garlic, minced	
3 Tbls. vegetable oil	**1 Tbls. canola oil or less*
3 cups vegetables	**3 - 4 cups vegetables*
5 eggs lightly beaten	** ½ - ¾ cup Egg Beaters*
1 small slice of ham, chopped	**Use extra lean turkey ham*

Directions:

COOK the rice, broth, water, Worcestershire sauce, margarine, and garlic in a large pan. Set aside. Stir fry the vegetables in a non-stick pan with minimal oil or some cooking spray (add a little broth or wine to steam vegetables until crisp tender). Remove vegetables to a bowl and stir fry chopped ham slice and the *Egg Beaters* until eggs are cooked. Combine rice, eggs, and vegetables and heat through. Serve with a sprinkle of soy sauce. Makes 8 servings.

Nutritional Analysis:	Original	Lowfat Version
Kcals. =	353	246
Chol. =	140 mg	5 mg
Sodium =	1196 mg	408 mg
Fat =	12 grams	3 grams
Fat % =	31 %	12 %

SHIPWRECK STEW

Original Recipe:

4 medium potatoes, peeled and sliced
1 medium onion, sliced
1 ½ lbs. hamburger
1 can tomato soup
1 can chili with beans
½ cup uncooked Minute Rice
1 beef bouillon cube + 1 ½ cups water
¼ tsp. Worcestershire sauce

Alterations:

*6 unpeeled potatoes, sliced

*16 oz. lean ground turkey
*Use Healthy Request
*1 can no-salt stewed tomatoes, pureed

*Use low-sodium beef broth
*Use low-sodium Worcestershire sauce
* ½ cup canned, rinsed pinto beans
*1 Tbls. chili powder, 1 tsp. cumin,
    1 tsp. cilantro
*Mrs. Dash's Table Blend

Directions:

LAYER raw potatoes, onion, and lean ground turkey in a large 3-quart casserole dish; season layers with *Mrs. Dash's Table Blend* seasoning. Combine tomato soup, stewed tomato puree, broth, spices, Worcestershire sauce, and pinto beans. Pour over layered ingredients. Bake covered 2 hours at 350. Serves 6.

Nutritional Analysis:

	Original	Lowfat Version
Kcals. =	563	396
Chol. =	114 mg	52 mg
Sodium =	1149 mg	644 mg
Fat =	29 grams	12 grams
Fat % =	46 %	26 %

SPICY LASAGNA

Original Recipe:

1 lb. ground beef
1 chopped onion
16 oz. tomato sauce
12 oz. water
Salt and pepper to taste
½ tsp. garlic powder
½ tsp. nutmeg
½ tsp. allspice
2 tsp. Italian seasoning
1 Tbls. dried parsley
¼ tsp. cloves or 2 whole cloves
1 tsp. oregano
16 oz. Lasagna noodles
16 oz. Monterey Jack cheese
1 pint cottage cheese

Alterations:

*8 oz. ground turkey

*Use no-salt tomato sauce
*8 oz. water + 4 oz. red wine
*Omit salt

*16 oz. shredded lite Mozzarella cheese
*1 pint nonfat Ricotta cheese or 1%
  cottage cheese

Directions:

BROWN ground turkey and onion. Add tomato sauce, water, and spices; simmer 10 to 15 minutes. Cook noodles until barely tender. Alternate ingredients in three layers; noodles, Ricotta or cottage cheese, Mozzarella, and sauce (in that order). Bake at 350 for 30 to 45 minutes. Let stand for 10 minutes before serving. Serves 8. Add fresh green salad or vegetables and dip along with whole grain bread or rolls for a complete meal.

Nutritional Analysis:

	Original	Lowfat Version
Kcals. =	684	511
Chol. =	109 mg	53 mg
Sodium =	1177 mg	826 mg
Fat =	33 grams	15 grams
Fat % =	43 %	27 %

LASAGNA BELMONTE

Original Recipe:	Alterations:
1 ½ lbs. lean ground beef	**16 oz. spiced ground turkey (fennel, anise, crushed red pepper, thyme)*
1 onion, chopped	
1 clove garlic, minced	
3 Tbls. olive oil	**1 Tbls. olive oil*
16 oz. tomato sauce	**Use no-salt tomato sauce*
1 can tomato paste (6 oz.)	
½ cup each red wine and water	
1 tsp. oregano	
1 tsp. salt	**Omit salt, add 1 tsp. basil*
½ tsp. each sugar and pepper	
16 oz. Lasagna noodles, cooked	
2 cups Ricotta cheese	**Use lowfat or nonfat Ricotta*
8 oz. Mozzarella cheese, thinly sliced	**Use lowfat Mozzarella*
½ cup grated Parmesan cheese	

Directions:

SPICE ground turkey early in the day or one day ahead. Saute the onion and garlic in olive oil until tender. Add the ground turkey and brown; drain on a paper towel. Combine the tomato sauce, paste, wine, water, oregano, basil, pepper, and sugar. Add the drained turkey and simmer for about 1 ½ hours (you could get by with about 45 minutes).

MEANWHILE, cook, drain and rinse the noodles. Spray a 9X13 inch casserole dish. Spread a thin layer of sauce over the bottom. Arrange ⅓ of the noodles in an even layer over the sauce. Spread ⅓ cup of sauce over noodles; dot with ⅓ cup Ricotta, then cover with ⅓ of the sliced Mozzarella. Repeat this layering two more times. Sprinkle Parmesan cheese over top. If made ahead, cover and refrigerate. Bake, uncovered, in a 350 oven for about 40 - 60 minutes. Cut into 8 squares.

Nutritional Analysis:

	Original	Lowfat Version
Kcals. =	735	555
Chol. =	123 mg	61 mg
Sodium =	968 mg	554 mg
Fat =	36 grams	18 grams
Fat % =	44 %	29 %

CHICKEN OR TURKEY LASAGNA

Original Recipe:

*3 lbs. cooked chicken or turkey
    breast*
2 cups chicken broth
½ cup butter or margarine
1 lb. sliced mushrooms
½ cup dry white wine
½ tsp. tarragon leaves
4 Tbls. flour
1 tsp. salt
¼ tsp. each pepper and nutmeg
2 cups half and half

16 cooked Lasagna noodles
12 oz. shredded Swiss cheese

Alterations:

**4 cups chicken or turkey breast,
    cooked*
*Use low-sodium broth
*1 Tbls. olive oil
*Add 1 cup chopped onion

*3 - 4 Tbls. cornstarch
*Omit

**1 cup evaporated skim milk + 1 cup
    nonfat milk*

*Use lowfat cheese

Directions:

SAUTE mushrooms and onion in olive oil until limp. Add the wine and tarragon, reduce heat to medium and cook until pan juices have evaporated. Combine the evaporated skim milk, pepper, nutmeg, cornstarch, and broth; add to the vegetable mixture. Heat and cook, stirring, until smooth and thickened.

Spray a 9X13 casserole dish and spoon a thin layer of sauce over the bottom. Layer ⅓ of the noodles, ⅓ of chicken pieces, ⅓ sauce, and ⅓ cheese. Repeat layers two more times ending with cheese. Bake at 350 for about 40 - 50 minutes. Serves 8.

Nutritional Analysis:

	Original	Lowfat Version
Kcals. =	648	518
Chol. =	122 mg	76 mg
Sodium =	465 mg	179 mg
Fat =	24 grams	13 grams
Fat % =	35 %	23 %

POP'S
BARBECUE

This recipe was developed for my former Father-in-Law who always misses his "Texas Barbecue" when visiting the Pacific Northwest.

Original Recipe:

1 whole (about 5 lbs. including bone), thawed, skinned turkey breast (all fat removed)
1 cup smokey, thick, bottled barbecue sauce
Mrs. Dash's Extra Spicy *salt-free seasoning blend*

Directions:

COAT turkey breast with the barbecue sauce and place breast side down, in a slow-cooker. Season with *Mrs. Dash's* seasoning, and cook on low for 8 hours. Serve with additional warm barbecue sauce if desired. Makes 16 (4 oz.) servings.

Nutritional Analysis:

Kcals. =	135
Chol. =	65 mg
Sodium =	201 mg
Fat =	2 grams
Fat % =	13 %

SHEPHERD'S PIE

Original Recipe:

2 cups chopped onion
2 Tbls. margarine
1 lb. ground beef
½ cup beef broth
1 Tbls. catsup
¼ tsp. Worcestershire sauce
¼ tsp. prepared mustard
¼ tsp. salt
¼ tsp. pepper

Alterations:

*Omit
*12 - 16 oz. lean ground turkey
*Use low-sodium broth

*Use low-sodium Worcestershire

*Omit

Topping:

4 - 6 medium potatoes, mashed
¼ cup warm milk
3 Tbls. margarine
1 tsp. salt

*Use nonfat milk
*2 Tbls. diet margarine
*Omit or reduce to ¼ tsp.

Directions:

PREHEAT oven to 425. Saute the onion with the ground turkey; drain if necessary. Add remaining ingredients and place in a sprayed or non-stick 9 inch pan. Beat mashed potatoes with milk and margarine until light and fluffy. Spread over meat mixture, sealing edges. Bake for 30 minutes. Serve with a fresh green salad or hot California mix vegetables. Serves 4 - 6.

Nutritional Analysis:

	Original	Lowfat Version	
		12 oz. turkey (4 servings)	16 oz. turkey (6 servings)
Kcals. =	490	496	374
Chol. =	69 mg	59 mg	52 mg
Sodium =	1240 mg	407 mg	287 mg
Fat =	26 grams	15 grams	13 grams
Fat % =	47 %	27 %	30 %

SPAGHETTI PIE

Original Recipe:
6 oz. spaghetti
2 Tbls. margarine
⅓ cup Parmesan cheese, grated
2 whole eggs, beaten
1 lb. ground beef
½ cup chopped onions
¼ cup chopped green pepper
6 oz. tomato paste
1 tsp. sugar
1 tsp. dried oregano
½ tsp. garlic salt
1 cup cottage cheese

½ cup shredded Mozzarella cheese

Alterations:

*1 Tbls. diet margarine

* ½ cup Egg Beaters
*16 oz. lean ground turkey

* ½ tsp. garlic powder
*1 cup nonfat Quark or 1% lowfat
    cottage cheese
* ½ cup Truly Lite Mozzarella cheese

Directions:

COOK spaghetti and drain. Stir in margarine to coat warm spaghetti. Mix in Parmesan cheese and egg substitute. Form spaghetti mixture into a crust in a sprayed or non-stick 10 inch pie plate.

In a non-stick pan, cook the ground turkey, onion and green pepper until vegetables are tender. Stir in tomato paste, sugar, oregano and garlic powder. Heat through. Spread *Quark* or cottage cheese over spaghetti crust and top with meat and tomato mixture. Bake uncovered in a 350 oven for about 20 minutes. Sprinkle with Mozzarella cheese and bake 5 minutes longer. 6 servings.

Nutritional Analysis:

	Original	Lowfat Version
Kcals. =	482	400
Chol. =	151 mg	61 mg
Sodium =	590 mg	305 mg
Fat =	25 grams	15 grams
Fat % =	46 %	34 %

SWEDISH OR ITALIAN MEATBALLS

Original Recipe:

1 1/2 lbs. ground beef
1 egg
2 Tbls. parsley flakes

1 Tbls. Mrs. Dash's seasoning
1 tsp. garlic powder
3/4 cup oats

Alterations:

*1 lb. lean ground turkey
*2 egg whites
*2 Tbls. minced onion + 1 tsp. parsley flakes
*1 Tbls. Mrs. Dash's seasoning

*1 1/2 cups bread crumbs
* 1/3 cup nonfat milk

Directions:

MIX ground turkey and all remaining ingredients; form into about 18 medium meatballs and cook in the microwave for 10 minutes on high power. Makes 6 servings (3 meatballs per serving).

Nutritional Analysis:

	Original	Lowfat Version
Kcals. =	362	284
Chol. =	134 mg	54 mg
Sodium =	98 mg	272 mg
Fat =	23 grams	12 grams
Fat % =	57 %	38 %

NOTE: For Italian meatballs substitute mixed Italian spices for *Mrs. Dash's* seasonings and add 1/8 teaspoon minced dried garlic and 1/4 cup grated Parmesan cheese.

HAMBURGER PIE

Original Recipe:
2 Tbls. chopped onion
1 Tbls. shortening
1/2 lb. ground beef
1/8 tsp. pepper
1/4 tsp. salt
1/4 tsp. Accent

1 can (8 oz.) cut green beans
1/2 can tomato soup

1 cup mashed potatoes

1/4 tsp. paprika
1/2 cup shredded cheddar cheese

Alterations:
* 1/4 cup chopped onion
*Omit
* 1/2 lb. lean ground turkey

*Omit
*Or use Mrs. Dash's spices
* 1/4 cup bread crumbs
*1 egg white
*16 oz. frozen cooked green beans
*4 oz. no-salt tomato sauce + 1 Tbls.
    Worcestershire sauce
*4 servings mashed potatoes, made from
    instant (make with nonfat milk
    and 1 Tbls. diet margarine or
    Butter Buds)

* 1/2 cup lowfat shredded cheddar cheese

Directions:

COMBINE the ground turkey, onion, pepper, spices, bread crumbs and egg white.

Place in the bottom of a 9 or 10-inch quiche pan and microwave on high for about 6 to 8 minutes (cover while cooking); drain if necessary.

MIX the cooked green beans (or use mixed vegetables) with the tomato sauce and Worcestershire sauce; spoon over meat and top with prepared mashed potatoes.

SPRINKLE with cheese and bake at 350 for about 20 minutes. Makes 4 servings.

Nutritional Analysis:

	Original	Lowfat Version
Kcals. =	335	321
Chol. =	65 mg	46 mg
Sodium =	1048 mg	274 mg
Fat =	22 grams	12 grams
Fat % =	59 %	34 %

MANICOTTI

Original Recipe:

1 lb. ground beef +
    1 lb. ground Italian sausage
28 oz. canned tomatoes
12 oz. tomato paste
2 cups water
1 Tbls. brown sugar
1 tsp. oregano + ½ tsp. basil
1 clove minced garlic
2 cups shredded Mozzarella cheese
½ cup Parmesan cheese
1 cup chopped onion
½ cup soft bread crumbs
1 Tbls. chopped parsley
1 tsp. salt + ⅛ tsp. pepper
8 oz. Manicotti noodles

Alterations:

*12 oz. ground turkey, spiced

*Use no-salt tomatoes

*2 cups lite Mozzarella

*Omit salt

Directions:

CUT UP tomatoes and combine with tomato paste, water, brown sugar, oregano, basil and garlic in a large sauce pan. Cover and cook slowly one hour (could be prepared in the slow cooker). Remove from heat and stir in one cup of the Mozzarella cheese and ¼ cup Parmesan cheese. Brown ground turkey and onion; drain if necessary. Add one cup Mozzarella cheese, bread crumbs, parsley, and pepper. Cook the Manicotti five or six at a time in boiling water for 3 minutes. Drain thoroughly.

FILL the manicotti with meat mixture and add any remaining mixture to the sauce. Place one cup sauce in the bottom of a 9X13 inch non-stick baking dish. Arrange filled Manicotti in a single layer over sauce. Top with remaining sauce and sprinkle with ¼ cup Parmesan cheese. Bake, covered, at 350 for 45 minutes. Let stand five minutes before cutting. Makes 8 servings.

Nutritional Analysis:

	Original	Lowfat Version
Kcals. =	585	364
Chol. =	119 mg	45 mg
Sodium =	1096 mg	302 mg
Fat =	29 grams	12 grams
Fat % =	44 %	30 %

EASY CHEESY MANICOTTI

Original Recipe:

3 cups Quark *or nonfat Ricotta*
1 cup Truly Lite *Mozzarella cheese*
½ cup grated Parmesan cheese
¼ cup Egg Beaters *or 2 egg whites*
2 Tbls. chopped parsley
¼ tsp. Italian seasoning

Alterations:

* ½ cup shredded lite Mozzarella

* ½ - 1 tsp. seasoning

Directions:

COMBINE all ingredients and mix well. Fill one 8 oz. package of dry Manicotti shells (14 shells), using a knife or teaspoon.

32 oz. bottled spaghetti sauce

½ cup water
1 cup Truly Lite *Mozzarella cheese*

*24 oz. no-salt tomato sauce + 6 oz.
   tomato paste
*Use part wine/part water
* ½ cup shredded lite Mozzarella
*1 Tbls. mixed Italian spices
*1 cup minced fresh onion
*1 clove minced garlic

Directions:

COMBINE tomato sauce, tomato paste, wine, water, spices, onion, and garlic in a saucepan and simmer for about 30 minutes. Pour half the sauce into the bottom of a 9X13 inch baking dish; arrange filled Manicotti in a single layer. Cover evenly with remaining sauce. Cover tightly with foil; bake 1 hour at 350. Uncover and top with ½ cup shredded cheese. Continue baking 5 minutes. Let stand 10 minutes before serving. Serves 4.

Nutritional Analysis:

	Original	Lowfat Version
Kcals. =	769	528
Chol. =	41 mg	26 mg
Sodium =	1777 mg	568 mg
Fat =	24 grams	10 grams
Fat % =	29 %	16 %

BEEF MUSHROOM BAKE

Original Recipe:	Alterations:
2 packages frozen chopped spinach thawed and drained	
1 lb. lean ground beef	*1 lb. lean ground turkey
1 large onion chopped	
1/2 lb. sliced or minced mushrooms	
1 cup lite sour cream	*1 cup nonfat yogurt
1/2 tsp. each oregano, basil, and thyme	
1/8 tsp. nutmeg	
1 cup lowfat cheddar cheese, shredded	
1 cup grated Parmesan cheese	* 1/2 cup Parmesan
4 cups cooked brown rice	*4 - 6 cups cooked brown rice

Directions:

SAUTE ground turkey and onions; add mushrooms and simmer 5 minutes. Remove from heat; stir in spinach, nonfat yogurt, and seasonings. Add 1/2 cup cheddar cheese, rice, and 1/4 cup Parmesan. Stir and place in a non-stick baking dish. Sprinkle with remaining cheeses, cover and bake for 20 - 30 minutes. Let sit for 10 minutes before serving. Serve with salad and bread. Serves 6.

Nutritional Analysis:

	Original	Lowfat Version
Kcals. =	539	514
Chol. =	94 mg	65 mg
Sodium =	496 mg	349 mg
Fat =	26 grams	17 grams
Fat % =	43 %	29 %

MEATLOAF

Original Recipe:

1 lb. ground beef

2 medium slices soft bread cubes
¾ - 1 cup milk
1 whole egg
¼ cup chopped onion
1 tsp. salt
¼ tsp. pepper
1 Tbls. catsup
2 tsp. Worcestershire sauce

Alterations:

*12 oz. lean ground turkey + 4 oz.
    extra lean ground beef
*2 slices cracked wheat bread cubes
* ¾ - 1 cup nonfat milk
*2 egg whites

*Omit

*Use low-salt catsup
*Use low-salt Worcestershire

Directions:

BEAT egg whites, milk and bread cubes until smooth. Add all remaining ingredients, form into a loaf shape or place in a loaf pan and bake uncovered for about 1 hour at 350. Serves 4.

Nutritional Analysis:

	Original	Lowfat Version
Kcals. =	430	313
Chol. =	163 mg	75 mg
Sodium =	1094 mg	327 mg
Fat =	28 grams	15 grams
Fat % =	59 %	45 %

OLD FASHIONED MEATLOAF

Original Recipe:

2 lbs. hamburger

1 lb. ground pork
2 eggs
1 Tbls. Worcestershire
2 - 3 Tbls. dried parsley
½ green pepper, chopped
½ red pepper, chopped
1 medium onion, chopped
2 tsp. hot sauce
3 tsp. garlic powder
2 tsp. salt
2 tsp. pepper
14 oz. tomatoes

8 oz. tomato sauce

Alterations:

*2 lbs. ground turkey (spice with 1 tsp.
    each anise, fennel, thyme, sage)
*Omit
*4 egg whites
*Use low-sodium brand

*Omit salt

*Use no-salt brand
    (or stewed tomatoes)
*Use no-salt tomato sauce
*2 cups dried bread crumbs

Directions:

PUREE tomatoes and tomato sauce with peppers and onion. Add spices and combine with all other ingredients. Shape into a loaf and place in a 9X13 baking pan (there will be room on each side of the meatloaf for carrots and potatoes). Top meatloaf with some catsup. Cover with foil and bake at 350 for about 1 ½ hours. Makes 8 servings.

Nutritional Analysis:

	Original	Lowfat Version
Kcals. =	564	387
Chol. =	201 mg	80 mg
Sodium =	1049 mg	351 mg
Fat =	39 grams	17 grams
Fat % =	62 %	40 %

QUICK SPAGHETTI SAUCE

Original Recipe:

1 lb. hamburger

8 oz. pasta, cooked
24 oz. tomato sauce
1 package sauce mix

Alterations:

*6 oz. lean ground beef +
    6 oz. ground turkey
*16 oz. pasta, cooked
*32 oz. no-salt brand
*2 Tbls. mixed Italian spices
*1 cup sliced mushrooms
* 1/2 cup green pepper
* 1/2 cup chopped onion
* 1/3 cup wine
*6 oz. tomato paste

Directions:

BROWN beef and turkey; drain thoroughly. Saute mushrooms, green pepper, and onion in a few tablespoons of wine. Combine tomato sauce, paste, remaining wine, spices, and meat; place all in a slow cooker and simmer all day on low heat. Prepare pasta and serve with sauce. Makes 4 - 6 servings.

Nutritional Analysis:

	Original	Lowfat Version
Kcals. =	596	773
Chol. =	101 mg	66 mg
Sodium =	1338 mg	160 mg
Fat =	25 grams	17 grams
Fat % =	38 %	19 %

NOTE: If you use 100 % lean ground turkey, fat & kcalories will be reduced much further. Total kcals. are higher for the lowfat version because of the extra pasta.

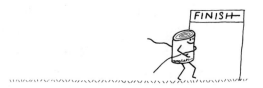

CALICO BEANS

Original Recipe:

16 oz. kidney beans, drained
16 oz. butter beans, drained
30 oz. canned pork and beans

1 lb. ground beef
½ lb. bacon
1 cup chopped onion

2 Tbls. vinegar
½ cup barbecue sauce
Liquid smoke

Alterations:

*Select a low-salt brand
*Use frozen lima beans
*20 oz. navy beans cooked from dry +
     6 oz. tomato paste, 2 oz.
     concentrated apple juice, 1 Tbls.
     brown sugar
*8 oz. ground turkey, cooked
*4 oz. Canadian bacon
*Plus ½ cup each chopped green and
     red pepper

Directions:

COMBINE all ingredients in a slow cooker and cook on low all day. Makes 4 main dish servings.

Nutritional Analysis:	Original	Lowfat Version
Kcals. =	1094	705
Chol. =	161 mg	53 mg
Sodium =	2511 mg	894 mg
Fat =	52 grams	12 grams
Fat % =	42 %	15 %

BEEF STEW

Original Recipe:

1 lb. stew meat
6 large potatoes, quartered
5 carrots, sliced
1 large onion, quartered
10 oz. frozen peas
2 packets stew seasoning mix

Oil
Water

Alterations:

*Cut off all visible fat

*1 cup each sliced celery and onion

**Garlic powder, pepper, lite
   Worcestershire sauce, other herbs
   as desired*
*Omit oil, substitute red wine
*Use low-sodium beef broth

Directions:

SAUTE meat in a non-stick Dutch oven coated with cooking spray (this step is optional; you could simply place the meat in the bottom of a slow-cooker with all the other ingredients except the peas). Drain the meat if necessary. Add about ½ cup wine, 2 - 3 cups of low-sodium beef broth, potatoes, carrots, celery, onions, herbs, spices, and 2 teaspoons of low-sodium Worcestershire. Simmer for about 2 ½ hours (or all day if using a slow-cooker). Add the frozen peas about 30 minutes before serving. If you like a thicker gravy, combine about 2 - 3 tablespoons of cornstarch with a small amount of the broth and thicken right before you add the peas. Makes 6 servings.

Nutritional Analysis:

	Original	Lowfat Version
Kcals. =	576	502
Chol. =	80 mg	80 mg
Sodium =	1016 mg	266 mg
Fat =	12 grams	18 grams
Fat % =	28 %	22 %

*Although the original recipe was fairly low in fat, it was excessively high in sodium.

CLASSIC BEEF STROGANOFF

Original Recipe:

16 oz. beef tenderloin or sirloin
    1 inch thick
2 Tbls. butter or margarine
½ lb. mushrooms, sliced
1 medium onion, minced
2 Tbls. catsup
10 ¾ oz. condensed beef broth
1 clove minced garlic
1 tsp. salt
3 Tbls. flour
1 cup sour cream
3 - 4 cups cooked noodles

Alterations:

*12 oz. lean round steak
*Omit - use a non-stick pan

*2 - 3 packets low-sodium broth + water

*Omit
*Or cornstarch
*1 cup lowfat or nonfat yogurt
*6 cups cooked non-egg pasta

Directions:

SAUTE cubed round steak in a non-stick pan with a little of the broth along with the mushrooms, onion, and garlic. Add the remaining beef broth and catsup; simmer until meat is tender (this recipe could also be prepared in the slow-cooker). Mix flour or cornstarch with a little wine or broth and stir into hot meat mixture. Simmer until thickened. Stir yogurt into mixture right before serving. Warm but do not boil after adding yogurt. Serve over hot cooked pasta. Serves 4.

Nutritional Analysis:

	Original	Altered Version
Kcals. =	675	549
Chol. =	178 mg	74 mg
Sodium =	1209 mg	192 mg
Fat =	16 grams	9 grams
Fat % =	41 %	16 %

QUICK TURKEY STROGANOFF

Original Recipe:

16 oz. ground turkey
1 cup chopped onions
½ lb. sliced fresh mushrooms
1 clove garlic, minced
1 can cream of mushroom soup
½ cup plain yogurt

½ cup lite sour cream
2 Tbls. catsup
2 tsp. Worcestershire sauce
½ tsp. black pepper
6 cups cooked pasta

Alterations:

*12 oz. ground turkey

*1 can Healthy Request mushroom soup
*1 cup nonfat yogurt (could use some
    Quark, also)
*Omit

*Use low-sodium Worcestershire

Directions:

SAUTE meat with vegetables and drain. Mix other ingredients well (except pasta).
Heat thoroughly but DO NOT boil. Combine with meat mixture. Serve over hot pasta
with green peas and tomatoes. Serves 6.

Nutritional Analysis:

	Original	Lowfat Version
Kcals. =	486	414
Chol. =	61 mg	40 mg
Sodium =	675 mg	466 mg
Fat =	18 grams	11 grams
Fat % =	33 %	24 %

MEATBALL STROGANOFF

Original Recipe:

1 ½ lbs. lean ground beef

1 small onion, chopped
¼ cup grated Parmesan cheese
⅓ cup milk
1 egg beaten
1 tsp. salt
1 tsp. Worcestershire sauce
Pepper
1 can cream mushroom soup
1 beef bouillon cube
4 oz. canned mushrooms
1 Tbls. margarine
½ cup sour cream
6 oz. rice, cooked

Alterations:

*12 oz. lean ground turkey + ½ cup
bread crumbs

*Use canned grated Parmesan
*Use skim milk
* ¼ cup egg substitute or 2 egg whites
*Omit
*Use low-sodium Worcestershire

*Use Healthy Request
*Use low-sodium
*1 cup sliced fresh mushrooms
*Use diet margarine
* ½ cup yogurt
*8 oz. rice, cooked

Directions:

MIX the ground turkey, onion, Parmesan cheese, milk, egg whites, Worcestershire sauce, bread crumbs, and pepper. Shape turkey mixture into small meatballs and brown on all sides over medium heat in a non-stick skillet sprayed with cooking spray. Reduce heat and simmer, adding a little wine or broth to prevent over-browning. Meanwhile, saute mushrooms in the diet margarine. Add the soup and beef broth packet; heat mixture thoroughly. Stir in yogurt and meatballs until smooth and creamy; do not boil. Serve immediately over hot cooked rice or pasta. Serves 4.

Nutritional Analysis:

	Original	Lowfat Version
Kcals. =	871	546
Chol. =	221 mg	66 mg
Sodium =	1903 mg	669 mg
Fat =	51 grams	19 grams
Fat % =	52 %	32 %

SWISS STEAK

Original Recipe:

¾ lb. extra lean top round steak
1 can cream of mushroom soup (use Campbell's Healthy Request)
2 cups beef broth (use low sodium)
1 cup chopped onions (or more if desired)
4 servings potatoes or pasta

Directions:

CUT steak into strips and flour lightly. Place steak, soup, broth, and onion into a shallow pan. Cover and cook on low (after bringing to a boil) for 1 to 1 ½ hours. Add water as needed.

SERVE over either non-egg pasta or potatoes. Makes 4 servings.

Nutritional Analysis: (as served with potatoes)

Kcals. =	488
Chol. =	71 mg
Sodium =	304 mg
Fat =	13 grams
Fat % =	24 %

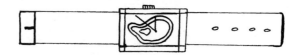

LAYERED ENCHILADA PIE

Original Recipe:

1 lb. ground beef
1 medium onion, chopped
1 clove minced garlic
2 Tbls. butter
¼ tsp. pepper
2 tsp. salt
⅔ cup water
1 Tbls. chili powder
4 ½ oz. chopped black olives
8 oz. tomato sauce
6 large flour tortillas

½ lb. shredded cheddar cheese

Alterations:

*12 oz. ground turkey

*Omit

*Omit

*Omit
*Use no-salt tomato sauce
*12 corn tortillas or 6 large whole wheat tortillas
*Use lowfat cheese

Directions:

BROWN ground turkey, onion and garlic. Add seasonings and tomato sauce. Use a casserole (non-stick) and alternate layers of tortillas, meat sauce, and cheese. Sprinkle ½ cup of the cheese on top. Add water, cover and bake in a 400 oven for 30 minutes. Remove lid the last 5 minutes to brown cheese. Serves 4.

Nutritional Analysis:

	Original	Lowfat Version
Kcals. =	914	539
Chol. =	174 mg	104 mg
Sodium =	2517 mg	685 mg
Fat =	56 grams	20 grams
Fat % =	54 %	33 %

CHILI

Original Recipe:	Alterations:
½ lb. lean ground beef	*Omit
½ lb. ground turkey	
1 onion, chopped	
¼ lb. sliced mushrooms	* ½ lb. sliced mushrooms
2 Tbls. currants	
15 ½ oz. low- salt garbanzo beans, drained	
16 oz. diced tomatoes	*16 oz. low-salt tomatoes, diced
8 oz. tomato sauce	*8 oz. low-salt tomato sauce
1 tsp. mustard	
2 tsp. chili powder	
¼ tsp. ground cloves	
1 bay leaf	

Directions:

SAUTE ground turkey, onions, and mushrooms; drain well. Add remaining ingredients and bring to a boil or place in a slow cooker. Simmer on the stove for one hour or on low in the slow cooker all day. Serve with salad and homemade tortilla chips or bread. Serves 4.

Nutritional Analysis:	Original	Lowfat Version
Kcals. =	543	397
Chol. =	89 mg	39 mg
Sodium =	657 mg	115 mg
Fat =	22 grams	12 grams
Fat % =	36 %	25 %

SOFT TURKEY TACOS

Original Recipe:

½ lb. thinly sliced roast beef
½ cup picante sauce
4 flour tortillas
4 Tbls. shredded cheddar cheese
4 sliced ripe olives
4 slices tomato
Sweet red pepper strips
4 Tbls. sour cream
4 Tbls. mashed avocado

Alterations:

* ½ lb. thinly sliced turkey breast

*4 whole wheat flour tortillas
*Use lowfat cheddar
*Omit

*4 Tbls. nonfat yogurt

Directions:

TOSS thinly sliced turkey breast with the picante sauce; divide between 4 whole wheat tortillas. Top meat with 1 tablespoon cheese, 1 slice tomato, red pepper strips, and combined (1 tablespoon each) yogurt and avocado. Makes 4 soft tacos. Serve with Mexican rice (see below) and baked tortilla chips with salsa.

Nutritional Analysis:

	Original	Lowfat Version
Kcals. =	341	304
Chol. =	55 mg	45 mg
Sodium =	499 mg	449 mg
Fat =	13 grams	9 grams
Fat % =	33 %	25 %

NOTE: To make Mexican rice simply cook 1 cup raw brown or white rice in a non-stick pan for 30 minutes (or until all liquid is absorbed and rice is tender) with the following ingredients: 1 cup tomato juice, 1 cup water, and 1 tsp. canola oil. Stir in 2 - 4 tablespoons salsa or picante sauce during last 5 minutes of cooking time. Makes 4 - 6 servings.

BURRITOS

Original Recipe:

1 can refried beans (no lard)
1 lb. ground turkey
½ onion, chopped
½ tsp. chili powder
½ tsp. cumin
⅛ to ¼ cup currants

Alterations:

*1 ½ cans no-fat refried beans
*8 oz. ground turkey

*1 tsp. chili powder
*1 tsp. cumin
*Or use ¼ cup raisins, chopped

Directions:

BROWN the ground turkey and onion; drain if necessary. Combine refried beans, meat mixture, chili powder, cumin, and currants. Mix well and set aside.

10 whole wheat tortillas
1 ½ cups shredded lowfat cheddar or Jack cheese
Melted diet margarine

*Omit diet margarine - mix 1 can
  pureed stewed tomatoes with 1 tsp.
  each chili powder and cumin

Directions:

WARM thawed tortillas in the package for about 1 minute in the microwave. Place ⅓ cup filling on the center of the tortilla; sprinkle with 1 tablespoon cheese and fold tortillas to completely enclose filling. Place tortillas in two shallow baking pans (spray with non-stick coating or use non-stick pans). Top tortillas with about 2 heaping tablespoons of the tomato sauce and sprinkle with the remaining cheese. Bake at 400 for 15 to 20 minutes. Serve with lettuce, salsa, and chopped tomatoes. Enjoy homemade fat-free corn tortilla chips and salsa prior to serving the burritos. YUM! Serves 5 (will serve 8 to 10 if Mexican rice and a tossed green salad are served as side dishes). See bottom of page 53 for Mexican rice recipe.

Nutritional Analysis:

	Original	Lowfat Version
Kcals. =	564	509
Chol. =	84 mg	55 mg
Sodium =	627 mg	545 mg
Fat =	25 grams	18 grams
Fat % =	39 %	31 %

NOTE: If you decide to leave the meat out all together, simply use two cans of refried beans = 534 Kcals., 24 mg Chol., 13 grams Fat, 21 % Fat.

ENCHILADAS

Original Recipe:	Alterations:
1 ½ lb. to 2 lbs. ground beef	*12 oz. lean ground turkey
12 flour tortillas	*12 corn or whole wheat tortillas
1 cup sour cream	* ½ cup nonfat yogurt
¼ cup chili powder	*2 Tbls. chili powder
32 oz. tomato sauce	*32 oz. low-salt tomato sauce
½ tsp. ground coriander	
Bay leaf	
½ tsp. oregano	
2 cubes beef bouillon	*2 packets low-sodium beef bouillon
2 Tbls. bacon fat	*Omit
1 Tbls. flour	*1 Tbls. cornstarch
8 oz. shredded cheddar cheese	*8 oz. lowfat cheddar cheese

Directions:

COMBINE cornstarch, bouillon, tomato sauce, coriander, bay leaf, oregano, and chili powder; simmer for 10 minutes. Saute ground turkey and onion; add pepper, all but ½ cup shredded cheese, and the nonfat yogurt.

SOFTEN tortillas in the microwave and fill each one with equal amounts of meat mixture; roll them up and place in a shallow non-stick baking dish. Before baking, pour sauce over enchiladas, sprinkle with remaining cheese and bake at 350 for about 20 minutes. Serves 6.

Nutritional Analysis:

	Original	Lowfat Version
Kcals. =	875	382
Chol. =	184 mg	60 mg
Sodium =	1915 mg	592 mg
Fat =	53 grams	12 grams
Fat % =	55 %	26 %

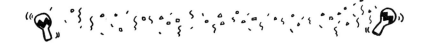

SPICY CHICKEN AND SPINACH ENCHILADAS

Original Recipe:

3 cups cubed cooked chicken
1 ¼ cup hot picante sauce
1 cup chopped green onions
½ cup chopped red bell pepper
16 oz. tomato sauce
3 cups shredded cheddar cheese
10 oz. frozen spinach, thawed and drained
4 ¼ oz. olives
4 oz. green chilies
1 clove garlic
¾ tsp. salt
⅛ tsp. pepper
10 (8-inch) flour tortillas
Garnish with shredded lettuce, chopped
    tomatoes, and sliced green onions
Dairy sour cream

Alterations:

*3 cups cooked chicken breast, cubed

*Use low sodium brand
*2 cups shredded lowfat cheddar cheese

*Omit

*Omit

*Use whole wheat tortillas

*Use nonfat yogurt (optional)

Directions:

IN A 4-QUART SAUCEPAN, combine the chicken, ¾ cup picante sauce, the onions, red pepper, 8 oz. of tomato sauce, 1 cup cheese, spinach, chilies, garlic, and pepper. Mix well and simmer uncovered over low heat about 20 minutes. Soften tortillas in microwave. Spray a 9X13 inch non-stick pan. Spoon about ½ cup chicken mixture down center of each tortilla. Roll up; place seam side down in one row down center of the pan. In a small pan combine remaining picante sauce and tomato sauce; mix well. Pour mixture evenly over enchiladas. Sprinkle with remaining cheese. Bake at 350 for about 25 - 30 minutes. Let stand 5 minutes. Serve with shredded lettuce, chopped tomato, and green onions (nonfat yogurt is optional). Makes 10 enchiladas (one or two per person depending upon what is served with the enchiladas). (Analysis based on one tortilla)

Nutritional Analysis:	Original	Lowfat Version
Kcals. =	413	297
Chol. =	77 mg	50 mg
Sodium =	1305 mg	667 mg
Fat =	22 grams	11 grams
Fat % =	46 %	31 %

EASY MEXICALI DINNER

Original Recipe:

1 lb. ground beef
½ cup chopped onion
16 oz. canned tomatoes
6 oz. noodles
6 oz. tomato paste
1 ½ cups cheddar cheese
½ cup olives

1 tsp. salt
¼ tsp. basil
⅛ tsp. pepper

Alterations:

*12 oz. lean ground turkey

*16 oz. low-sodium stewed tomatoes
*12 oz. noodles
*Plus 8 oz. low-sodium tomato sauce
*Use lowfat shredded cheddar
*Omit olives and add 4 oz. diced
    green chilies
*Omit salt; add 1 tsp. cumin
*1 tsp. basil

Directions:

COOK noodles and set aside. Brown ground turkey in a non-stick pan; drain if necessary. Add chopped onion, chilies, spices, tomato paste, tomato sauce, and stewed tomatoes. Simmer meat mixture for about 10 minutes. Add the cooked noodles and one cup of cheese; stir to combine and place in a non-stick casserole dish. Sprinkle top of casserole with remaining cheese and bake at 350 for about 20 minutes. Serves 4.

Nutritional Analysis:

	Original	Lowfat Version
Kcals. =	754	713
Chol. =	146 mg	88 mg
Sodium =	1364 mg	334 mg
Fat =	42 grams	23 grams
Fat % =	50 %	29 %

ENCHILADA PIE

Original Recipe:

2 lbs. ground beef
1 tsp. salt
1 medium onion, chopped
1 can tomato soup
20 oz. enchilada sauce
1 cup water
12 flour tortillas
2 cups shredded cheddar cheese

Alterations:

*12 oz. lean ground turkey
*Omit salt

*Use Healthy Request
*8 oz. no-salt tomato sauce + 12 oz. salsa

*15 corn tortillas
*8 oz. shredded Mozzarella or lite
    cheddar cheese

Directions:

SAUTE turkey and onion. Drain if necessary. Add soup, tomato sauce, salsa, and water. Simmer 5 minutes. Alternate mixture in a large casserole dish or slow cooker. Start with meat mixture, cheese, then 3 tortillas and continue alternating. Sprinkle remaining cheese on top. Microwave 10 minutes or cook in slow cooker on low until ready to serve (also can be baked in the oven at 350 for 20 - 30 minutes). Makes 6 servings.

Nutritional Analysis:

	Original	Lowfat Version
Kcals. =	884	481
Chol. =	176 mg	59 mg
Sodium =	1908 mg	513 mg
Fat =	52 grams	19 grams
Fat % =	52 %	34 %

TASTY TACO PIZZA

Original Recipe:

16 oz. ground beef

16 oz. tomato sauce
1 package taco seasoning mix

2 cans refrigerated crescent dinner rolls
½ lb. Velveeta *cheese*
1 cup chopped lettuce
½ cup chopped tomatoes
1 small can sliced ripe olives

Alterations:

*6 oz. ground turkey + ½ cup chopped onion
*Use no-salt tomato sauce
*1 Tbls. chili powder, 1 tsp. cumin 1 tsp. oregano, 1 tsp. cilantro
*Or use one loaf frozen bread dough or make your own dough
*4 oz. lowfat cheddar cheese, shredded
*2 cups chopped lettuce
*1 cup chopped tomatoes
*Omit olives
*14 oz. canned no-fat refried beans
*Salsa

Directions:

BROWN lean ground turkey and drain if necessary. Stir in tomato sauce, onion, and spices; simmer 5 - 10 minutes. Press dough onto bottom and slightly up the sides of a non-stick 9X13 pan or a 12-15 inch pizza pan (if using refrigerated crescent rolls, seal all edges by pressing together with a fork). Warm refried beans and spread over unbaked crust. Top with the meat mixture and the shredded cheddar cheese; bake at 375 for about 20 minutes. Top with lettuce and tomato, and serve with salsa. Makes 4 - 8 servings.

Nutritional Analysis:	Original	Lowfat Version	w/bread dough
	(8 servings)	(8 servings)	(4 servings)
Kcals. =	481	357	484
Chol. =	70 mg	25 mg	29 mg
Sodium =	1658 mg	1044 mg	952 mg
Fat =	26 grams	12 grams	11 grams
Fat % =	49 %	31 %	21 %

POACHED SALMON WITH TARRAGON MAYONNAISE

Original Recipe:

2 carrots, chopped
2 stalks celery, chopped
1 cup chopped onion
1 tsp. pepper
½ tsp garlic powder
1 Tbls. dried parsley
16 oz. chicken broth
½ cup dry white wine
2 Tbls. lemon juice
12 oz. fresh salmon
½ tsp. tarragon
½ cup mayonnaise
2 tsp. lemon juice
½ tsp. lemon peel

Alterations:

*Use low-sodium broth

*Use nonfat mayonnaise

Directions:

CHOP all vegetables and place in broth, white wine, and lemon juice. Add pepper, garlic powder, and parsley to broth mixture. Bring liquid to a boil and reduce heat. Place salmon in liquid and simmer until fish flakes easily when tested with a fork. Serve warm or cold with tarragon mayonnaise. Mayonnaise mixture should be chilled for 2 - 4 hours before serving. Serves 4.

Nutritional Analysis:

	Original	Lowfat Version
Kcals. =	374	192
Chol. =	61 mg	45 mg
Sodium =	601 mg	473 mg
Fat =	26 grams	4 grams
Fat % =	65 %	18 %

CRAB LINGUINI

Original Recipe:

¼ lb. butter
1 egg yolk
¼ cup heavy cream
½ cup Parmesan cheese
1 tsp. garlic powder
1 lb. cooked crab meat

1 lb. egg noodles
¼ tsp. pepper
¼ tsp. salt

Alterations:

*2 Tbls. diet margarine
* ½ cup egg substitute
* ½ cup evaporated skim milk

* ½ lb. cooked crab meat or imitation crab
*1 lb. Linguini pasta

*Omit salt

Directions:

COMBINE margarine, egg substitute, skim milk, cheese, garlic, and pepper. Prepare pasta; drain and mix with egg mixture over low heat. Fold in cooked crab meat and let stand until warmed throughout. Serves 4 generously. Tossed green salad or hot mixed vegetables plus a whole grain roll or bread makes this a complete meal (even this scaled-down version is very rich tasting). 4 servings.

Nutritional Analysis:

	Original	Lowfat Version
Kcals. =	564	323
Chol. =	251 mg	45 mg
Sodium =	866 mg	517 mg
Fat =	37 grams	9 grams
Fat % =	57 %	22 %

HALIBUT SUPREME

Original Recipe:

12 oz. halibut or cod
¼ cup chopped green onion
6 oz. shrimp (canned or fresh)
1 cup milk
2 Tbls. butter
2 Tbls. flour
1 cup shredded cheddar cheese
4 Tbls. shredded cheddar cheese
½ tsp. paprika

Alterations:

*1 cup skim milk
*Omit
*1 Tbls. cornstarch
* ¼ cup grated Parmesan cheese
*4 Tbls. shredded lowfat cheddar cheese
*Plus ¼ tsp. each Worcestershire and
   dry mustard

Directions:

PLACE fish in a sprayed or non-stick pan. Sprinkle with chopped green onion. Drain and pour the can of shrimp over fish. Make a cheese sauce by mixing the skim milk with the cornstarch. Heat and stir until thickened; add Parmesan, Worcestershire, and dry mustard. Pour sauce over fish and sprinkle with paprika. Bake at 425 - 450 for about 15 minutes. Sprinkle with lowfat cheddar cheese and bake a few minutes longer until melted. Serves 4.

Nutritional Analysis:

	Original	Lowfat Version
Kcals. =	390	210
Chol. =	162 mg	109 mg
Sodium =	415 mg	291 mg
Fat =	22 grams	6 grams
Fat % =	52 %	25 %

SHRIMP STEW

Original Recipe:

3 lbs. fresh shrimp
¾ cup cooking oil
3 cups chopped onion
1 ½ cups chopped green onions
3 cups chopped celery
12 oz. tomato paste
1 tsp. salt
½ tsp. pepper
3 cups water
1 clove minced garlic
2 Tbls. Worcestershire sauce
6 cups cooked rice

Alterations:

*18 oz. fresh shrimp
*2 Tbls. olive oil

*Omit salt

*Use low-salt Worcestershire sauce
*Use half brown rice (or pasta)

Directions:

SAUTE the onion, green onion, garlic and celery in the olive oil (add 1 tablespoon wine if more liquid is required). Combine tomato paste, pepper, water, garlic, and Worcestershire sauce in a slow cooker; add the sauted vegetables to the tomato mixture. Cook over low heat 4 - 8 hours. Add cooked shrimp or other cooked seafood or surimi during the last 30 minutes to one hour. Serve over hot cooked rice or pasta. Serves 6.

Nutritional Analysis:

	Original	Lowfat Version
Kcals. =	753	408
Chol. =	442 mg	166 mg
Sodium =	1311 mg	468 mg
Fat =	31 grams	8 grams
Fat % =	37 %	16 %

SEAFOOD
STEW

Original Recipe:

1 ½ tsp. olive oil
½ cup chopped onions
½ cup chopped fresh parsley (or 2 Tbls. dried)
3 small red potatoes, cubed
⅓ lb. white fish (cod, snapper)
¼ lb. scallops
¼ lb. salad shrimp
8 -10 clams
12 oz. canned tomato juice (use low sodium variety and add some spices for flavor)
4 fresh tomatoes, chopped
10 large shrimp
1 clove garlic minced

Directions:

SAUTE onion, garlic, and parsley in olive oil; add to a slow cooker with all remaining ingredients EXCEPT seafood. Cook on low all day. Microwave seafood until barely cooked and add to slow cooker shortly before serving. Serve with hot whole grain rolls and salad. Serves 4 generously. (Other vegetables could also be added to this stew)

Nutritional Analysis:

Kcals. =	276
Chol. =	111 mg
Sodium =	487 mg
Fat =	4 grams
Fat % =	12 %

SALMON QUICHE

Original Ingredients:

Alterations:

Crust:

1 cup whole wheat flour
2/3 cup shredded sharp cheddar cheese
1/4 cup chopped almonds
1/3 tsp. salt
1/4 tsp. paprika
6 Tbls. corn oil

*1 oz. shredded lite sharp cheddar cheese
* 1/8 cup chopped almonds
* 1/8 tsp. salt, optional

*2 Tbls. canola oil + 4 Tbls. water

Directions:

COMBINE and set aside 1/3 of the above mixture; press remaining mixture into a 10-inch pie or quiche pan (non-stick or lightly sprayed). Bake at 400 for 10 minutes.

Filling:

15 oz. canned salmon
3 beaten eggs
1/2 cup shredded sharp cheddar cheese
1/4 cup mayonnaise
1 Tbls. grated onion
3 drops hot pepper sauce
1/4 tsp. dill weed
1 cup sour cream

*Or use leftover fresh baked salmon
* 3/4 cup Egg Beaters
*1 oz. shredded lite sharp cheddar cheese
*Use nonfat mayonnaise

*1 cup nonfat yogurt

Directions:

DRAIN salmon reserving liquid; add water to make 1/2 cup. Flake (and clean if using canned) and combine with *Egg Beaters*, nonfat yogurt, mayonnaise, and liquid. Stir in cheese, onion, dill, and hot pepper sauce and pour all into the baked crust. Sprinkle with remaining crust mixture. Bake quiche at 325 for 45 minutes. Makes 6 servings.

Nutritional Analysis:

	Original	Lowfat Version
Kcals. =	600	301
Chol. =	194 mg	48 mg
Sodium =	837 mg	608 mg
Fat =	47 grams	13 grams
Fat % =	69 %	38 %

SCALLOPS WITH SPINACH

Original Recipe:

1 lb. fresh or frozen scallops
3 sweet yellow peppers
3 sweet red peppers
2 Tbls. margarine
1 clove garlic, minced
4 cups spinach
½ cup whipping cream
2 Tbls. tomato paste
1 Tbls. lemon juice
¼ tsp. salt + ¼ tsp. pepper

Alterations:

*2 Tbls. diet margarine

* ½ cup evaporated skim milk

*Omit salt

Directions:

THAW scallops. Rinse scallops and pat dry; halve large ones. Slice peppers lengthwise into ½ inch strips. In a large non-stick pan, saute peppers and garlic until tender in the margarine. Add spinach and stir-fry 30 seconds more until wilted. Spoon atop 4 plates. Cover and keep warm. To the same skillet add the evaporated skim milk and tomato paste. Bring to boiling; add scallops. Simmer, uncovered, 3 to 4 minutes or until scallops are opaque. With a slotted spoon, arrange scallops atop vegetables. Bring cream mixture to boiling. Whisk briskly for one minute or until slightly thickened. Add lemon juice and ¼ tsp. pepper. Spoon over scallops. Serves 4.

Nutritional Analysis:

	Original	Lowfat Version
Kcals. =	306	202
Chol. =	78 mg	39 mg
Sodium =	475 mg	339 mg
Fat =	18 grams	4 grams
Fat % =	53 %	18 %

SHRIMP
CURRY

Original Recipe:

12 large shrimp
1 cup water
12 oz. canned coconut milk
4 Tbls. vegetable oil
½ lb. potatoes

1 tsp. curry powder
¼ tsp. turmeric
¼ tsp. nutmeg
¼ tsp. cloves
¼ tsp. cardamom
¼ oz. half and half

Alterations:

*Use low-sodium beef or chicken broth
*3 oz. canned coconut milk
*1 tsp. canola oil
*1 lb. potatoes, cubed
*   +1 cup shredded carrot*
*   +1 cup chopped onion*
*   +1 clove garlic, minced*
*2 tsp. curry powder

*12 oz. evaporated skim milk + 2 Tbls.
*   cornstarch + 1 tsp. coconut flavoring*
*2 cups cooked chopped broccoli

Directions:

COMBINE the oil, spices, coconut milk and water; and bring to a boil. Add the potatoes, carrot, onion, and garlic; bring to a boil again and simmer for 25 minutes (add the shrimp and cooked broccoli during the last 10 - 15 minutes). Combine evaporated skim milk, coconut flavoring, and cornstarch; add to shrimp and potato mixture. Cook until slightly thickened. Serve with wheat rolls and a fruit salad. Makes 4 servings.

Nutritional Analysis: (curry sauce)	Original	Lowfat Version
Kcals. =	366	274
Chol. =	33 mg	45 mg
Sodium =	48 mg	412 mg
Fat =	33 grams	7 grams
Fat % =	77 %	22 %

POTATO VEGETABLE CASSEROLE

Original Recipe: Alterations:

2 lb. frozen hash brown potatoes
   (without added fat)
1/2 cup margarine, melted   *Omit
1/2 tsp. salt   *Omit
1/4 tsp. pepper
1 can cream of chicken soup   *Use Campbell's Healthy Request
1/2 cup chopped onion
16 oz. sour cream   *16 oz. nonfat yogurt
10 oz. shredded cheddar cheese   *5 oz. shredded lowfat cheddar
2 cups crushed corn flakes
1/4 cup melted margarine   *2 Tbls. melted diet margarine
                                          *Optional: 20 oz. frozen mixed
                                             vegetables such as
                                             Oriental Mix (onion,
                                             mushrooms, broccoli,
                                             and string beans)

Directions:

COMBINE potatoes and frozen vegetables; toss (in a large bowl) with remaining ingredients and place in a 9X13 non-stick pan. Top with cornflake crumbs that have been mixed with 2 tablespoons melted diet margarine. Bake uncovered at 350 for about 1 hour and 15 minutes. Serves 12.

NOTE: Serve this with acorn squash or sweet potatoes, a slice of turkey ham, plus Mississippi Fudge Cake for dessert. Excellent!

Nutritional Analysis:	Original	Lowfat Version
Kcals. =	364	151
Chol. =	44 mg	9 mg
Sodium =	781 mg	403 mg
Fat =	29 grams	4 grams
Fat % =	70 %	26 %

CHEESE AND MUSHROOM QUICHE

Original Recipe:

Crust:
1 cup flour
⅓ cup butter
3 Tbls. buttermilk

Filling:
6 oz. Swiss cheese
1 cup onions, chopped
¼ lb. sliced mushrooms
2 Tbls. butter
1 tsp. thyme + ⅛ tsp. pepper
4 whole eggs
1 ½ cup whole milk
3 Tbls. white flour
¼ tsp. dry mustard
1 tsp. paprika
¼ tsp. salt

Alterations:

*Half white/half wheat
*3 Tbls. diet margarine

*6 oz. lowfat Swiss cheese

*2 Tbls. wine

*1 cup Egg Beaters
*1 ½ cup nonfat milk

*Omit

Directions:

PREPARE crust and place in a 9-inch pie plate. Cover crust with grated Swiss cheese. Saute onion and mushrooms with thyme, pepper and wine; layer over cheese.

BEAT egg substitute, milk, flour and dry mustard; pour over mushroom layer. Sprinkle with paprika and bake at 375 for 40 - 45 minutes, or until set. Serves 4 to 6.

Nutritional Analysis:

	Original: 4 serv.	6 serv./	Lowfat: 4 serv.	6 serv.
Kcals. =	641	428	380	253
Chol. =	321 mg	214 mg	28 mg	19 mg
Sodium =	546 mg	364 mg	353 mg	235 mg
Fat =	41 g	28 g	13 g	9 g
Fat % =	58 %	58 %	31 %	31 %

SPICY SCALLOPED POTATOES

Original Recipe:

2 Tbls. butter
1 large green onion, chopped
1 clove garlic, minced
¼ tsp. dried red pepper flakes
2 pounds red new potatoes, cut into
    thin slices

½ tsp. salt
¼ tsp. pepper
1 ¾ cups half and half
1 cup milk
¾ cup shredded Swiss or Gruyere
    cheese
2 Tbls. grated Parmesan cheese

Alterations:

*1 - 2 Tbls. diet margarine

*Or use 2 lb. bag no-fat hash brown
    potatoes; thaw for 2 min. in
    microwave
*Omit

*1 ¾ cups evaporated skim milk
*Use nonfat milk + 1 Tbls. cornstarch
*Use lowfat cheese (3 oz.)

Directions:

PREHEAT oven to 400. Spray a 9X13 casserole dish. Saute green onion, garlic, red pepper flakes, and pepper in the diet margarine until onions are tender. Add the evaporated skim milk. Combine the nonfat milk with the cornstarch and add to the evaporated milk. Bring to a boil, stirring constantly. Remove from heat.

PLACE potatoes in casserole dish and pour milk mixture over potatoes. Sprinkle with cheese and bake 15 minutes. Reduce oven temperature to 350 and continue to bake for 45 minutes. Serve warm. Makes 6 servings.

Nutritional Analysis:

	Original	Lowfat Version
Kcals. =	374	295
Chol. =	56 mg	14 mg
Sodium =	340 mg	221 mg
Fat =	18 grams	5 grams
Fat % =	42 %	16 %

PASTA PRIMAVERA

Ingredients:

1 cup cooked broccoli flowerets
1 cup cooked asparagus
1 cup blanched snow peas
1 small zucchini, blanched
1 cup cooked frozen corn
1 Tbls. finely minced garlic
1 Tbls. olive oil
1 large tomato, diced
½ cup sliced mushrooms
½ cup shredded carrots
½ cup minced parsley or 2 Tbls. dried parsley
½ tsp. pepper
12 oz. dry linguini pasta

Sauce:
2 tsp. diet margarine
1 Tbls. cornstarch
1 cup skim milk
½ cup low sodium chicken broth
½ cup grated Parmesan cheese
1 tsp. dried basil

Directions:

SAUTE the tomatoes, mushrooms, carrot, garlic, parsley, and pepper in the olive oil and add to the other slightly cooked vegetables; set aside. Prepare sauce while pasta is cooking. Combine the cold skim milk with the cornstarch and add to the broth along with the margarine and basil; cook over medium heat until thickened. Stir in the cheese and serve over the hot noodles. Makes 4 generous servings.

NOTE: Other vegetables can be used depending on what you like but this particular combination is very colorful. Enjoy with hot whole grain bread!

Nutritional Analysis:

Kcals. =	539
Chol. =	9 mg
Sodium =	277 mg
Fat =	10 grams
Fat % =	16 %

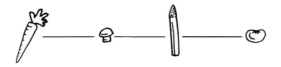

CHEESE POTATO CASSEROLE

Original Recipe:
2 Tbls. chopped onion
5 Tbls. butter or margarine
3 Tbls. flour
¼ tsp. paprika
1 ⅛ cup milk
1 cup shredded cheddar cheese
12 small cooked and peeled potatoes
1 tsp. salt

Alterations:
* ¼ cup chopped onion
*3 Tbls. diet margarine
*1 ½ - 2 Tbls. cornstarch

*1 ⅛ cup nonfat milk
*1 cup lowfat cheddar cheese, shredded
*Use white potatoes/do not peel
*Omit salt and use other seasonings

Directions:
SAUTE the onion in the diet margarine until tender; combine milk, cornstarch, and paprika and add to the onion mixture. Stir over medium heat until thickened. Remove from heat and blend in the cheese. Place cooked, sliced potatoes in a sprayed 1 ½ quart casserole. Pour the cheese sauce over the top and bake at 350 for 20 to 25 minutes. Serves 6.

Nutritional Analysis:

	Original	Lowfat Version
Kcals. =	437	339
Chol. =	52 mg	11 mg
Sodium =	590 mg	207 mg
Fat =	18 grams	6 grams
Fat % =	36 %	16 %

BROCCOLI CHEESE QUICHE

Original Recipe:

2 medium potatoes, thinly sliced
10 oz. frozen chopped broccoli, thawed
2/3 cup green onion, chopped
2 oz. sliced pimento
4 egg whites + 1 whole egg
1/3 cup plain lowfat yogurt
1/4 cup lowfat milk
1/2 tsp. basil
1/8 tsp. garlic powder
1/2 cup Mozzarella cheese, shredded
1/4 cup grated Parmesan cheese
2 oz. lowfat cream cheese

Alterations:

*Optional
* 3/4 cup Egg Beaters
*Use nonfat yogurt
*Use nonfat milk

*Use Truly Lite *Mozzarella*

*Use nonfat

Directions:

IN A NON-STICK SKILLET sprayed with cooking spray, cook potatoes until tender (10 - 15 minutes). Arrange potatoes over the bottom and around the sides of a 9-inch quiche pan (sprayed with vegetable cooking spray). Overlap the potatoes to form a decorative edge. Cook broccoli with the onion until tender. Drain well. Chop pimentos. Combine egg substitute, yogurt, milk, basil, garlic, pimento, Mozzarella cheese, and 2 tablespoons Parmesan cheese. Sprinkle top of quiche with remaining Parmesan. Drop cream cheese in chunks over the top. Cover with foil and bake at 375 for 10 minutes. Remove foil and bake 15 minutes longer. Let stand 10 minutes before serving. Garnish with pimento strips and fresh basil. Serves 6.

Nutritional Analysis:

	Original	Lowfat Version
Kcals. =	162	135
Chol. =	54 mg	9 mg
Sodium =	207 mg	205 mg
Fat =	7 grams	3 grams
Fat % =	36 %	20 %

QUICHE

Original Recipe:

½ cup cracker crumbs
½ cup Wheat Chex *crumbs*

¼ cup melted diet margarine
1 cup chopped onions, sauted
1 cup shredded Swiss cheese
1 cup shredded lowfat Monterey Jack
½ cup Egg Beaters
⅜ cup nonfat yogurt
⅜ cup lite sour cream
¼ tsp. nutmeg
1 package frozen spinach, thawed, well drained (or 10 - 16 oz. any frozen mixed vegetables).

Alterations:

* ½ cup each wheat germ & raw oats
*1 cup wheat bread crumbs +¼ cup
    whole wheat flour
*Plus ¼ cup nonfat milk & 1 tsp. basil

*2 oz. shredded fresh Parmesan cheese
*Or 1 cup shredded lite Mozzarella

* ¾ cup nonfat yogurt
*Omit

Directions:

MIX crumbs, wheat germ, raw oats, margarine, basil, and milk. Press into a sprayed 10-inch quiche pan. Bake at 350 for 8 minutes. Spray a non-stick saucepan and saute onions. Combine *Egg Beaters*, nutmeg, yogurt, 1 cup Mozzarella cheese, spinach, and onions. Put filling in pre-cooked crumb crust. Sprinkle with the shredded Parmesan cheese. Bake at 375 for 35 minutes. Let stand about 10 minutes before serving. Serves 4 - 6. Serve this with whole wheat nonfat crumpets w/jam and a fruit salad (peaches, pineapple, bananas). Also, 8 oz. chopped broccoli + 8 oz. sliced carrots, could be used instead of the spinach.

Nutritional Analysis:

	Original	Lowfat Version
Kcals. =	278	291
Chol. =	34 mg	12 mg
Sodium =	422 mg	525 mg
Fat =	15 grams	8 grams
Fat % =	49 %	24 %

CHINESE STIR-FRY

Original Recipe:

1 lb. baby carrots, pared and trimmed
1 jar baby corn
1 lb. mushrooms, fresh
2 red peppers, sliced
3 Tbls. minced scallions
1 Tbl. minced fresh ginger
2 cloves garlic, minced
¾ cup chicken broth (use low sodium brand)
2 ½ tsp. cornstarch
2 ½ tsp. Chinese black vinegar or any rice vinegar
2 tsp. oyster sauce
2 tsp. oil

Directions:

SAUTE peppers, mushrooms, scallions, garlic and carrots in the 2 tsp. oil. Combine oyster sauce, vinegar, cornstarch, chicken broth and ginger; add to vegetables when they are still crisp but tender. Stir until thickened and add the baby corn; heat until mixture is hot. Serve with hot sticky rice or Chinese noodles. 4 servings.

Nutritional Analysis:

Kcals. =	162
Chol. =	0 mg
Sodium =	328 mg
Fat =	4 grams
Fat % =	19 %

FETTUCCINI ALFREDO

Ingredients:

1 Tbls. diet margarine or ½ Tbls. olive oil
¼ cup chopped green onion
1 - 2 cloves minced garlic
1 Tbls. cornstarch
12 oz. evaporated skim milk
½ cup grated Parmesan cheese (or a mixture of Parmesan and Romano)
½ tsp. thyme
½ tsp. basil
¼ tsp. dill
6 cups cooked non-egg Fettuccini pasta

Directions:

SAUTE the garlic and onion in the margarine or olive oil for about 2 minutes. Combine the milk and cornstarch and add to the sauted onion along with herbs. Cook over medium heat, stirring frequently, until thickened. Remove from heat and stir in the cheese. Serve over the hot pasta with a fresh green salad and whole grain bread. Makes 4 servings.

Nutritional Analysis:

Kcals. =	431
Chol. =	13 mg
Sodium =	300 mg
Fat =	6 grams
Fat % =	13 %

SUMMER PIZZA

Original Recipe:

1 loaf frozen white bread dough
¼ cup olive oil
1 clove garlic, minced
3 large tomatoes, sliced thinly
1 bunch fresh basil leaves, washed
    and stemmed
1 can artichoke hearts (not marinated)
½ lb. Mozzarella cheese

Alterations:

*Use whole wheat if available
*2 Tbls. olive oil

*Use lite Mozzarella

Directions:

THAW dough according to instructions on the package. Spread on non-stick or sprayed pizza pan and let rise again for 15 minutes. Mix oil and garlic. Brush dough with oil mixture. Arrange tomato slices, basil leaves, and artichoke hearts on dough. Cover with shredded or sliced Mozzarella. Bake at 400 for 20 minutes or until dough is browned. Serves 4.

Nutritional Analysis:

	Original	Lowfat Version
Kcals. =	667	624
Chol. =	32 mg	30 mg
Sodium =	447 mg	483 mg
Fat =	24 grams	18 grams
Fat % =	33 %	26 %

WESTERN CHILI SOUP

Original Recipe:

1 ½ lbs. ground beef
1 cup chopped onion
2 ¼ tsp. garlic powder
1 cup beef broth
2 cans tomato soup
10 ¾ oz. water
2 (15 ½ oz.) cans kidney beans, undrained

3 cups cooked macaroni
3 Tbls. chili powder
2 Tbls. vinegar

Alterations:

*16 oz. lean ground turkey

*Use low-sodium broth
*Use Healthy Request

*Drain and rinse kidney beans; add
    15 oz. of no-salt tomato sauce

Directions:

SAUTE ground turkey, onion and garlic. Add remaining ingredients. Simmer 30 minutes stirring occasionally. Makes 12 cups or 6 servings.

Nutritional Analysis:

	Original	Lowfat Version
Kcals. =	648	534
Chol. =	102 mg	52 mg
Sodium =	1500 mg	605 mg
Fat =	27 grams	13 grams
Fat % =	37 %	22 %

HAM SOUP

Original Recipe:

2 cups chopped turkey ham
3 - 4 sliced carrots
1/2 cup sliced celery
1/2 cup chopped onion
1/2 cup chopped green pepper
6 - 8 small red potatoes
Water to cover (about 6 cups)
2 bay leaves
Pepper to taste

Directions:

SIMMER all on low until vegetables are tender or cook on low in a slow cooker all day (make one day ahead if not using a slow cooker). Serve with whole grain bread or rolls. 4 servings.

Nutritional Analysis:

Kcals. =	360
Chol. =	64 mg
Sodium =	1142 mg (using less ham and more vegetables will reduce sodium)
Fat =	6 grams
Fat % =	16 %

CREAMY CRAB SOUP

Original Recipe:
16 oz. cooked crab meat
2 Tbls. butter

1 cup chopped onion

½ - 1 cup shredded carrot
8 oz. cognac or sweet white wine
White and cayenne pepper to taste
4 cups heavy cream

4 Tbls. grated Parmesan cheese
2 oz. Gruyere cheese, shredded

Alterations:
*Or imitation crab
**2 Tbls. diet margarine + 1 clove
    minced garlic*
**Or combination of leek, shallot,
    and onion*
*1 ½ cups or 1 large carrot

**4 cups evaporated skim milk +
    1 - 2 Tbls. cornstarch*
*2 Tbls. grated Parmesan cheese
**1 oz. Gruyere or lowfat Swiss cheese,
    shredded or cubed*
* 2 cups cooked broccoli flowerets

Directions:

SAUTE onion, garlic, and carrot in margarine in a non-stick sauce pan until tender (add a tablespoon of the wine if necessary). Add the crab and wine, warming gently. Add the seasonings. Combine the evaporated skim milk with the cornstarch and stir into the crab mixture. Heat and stir until hot. Add cheeses and serve immediately. Serves 8.

Nutritional Analysis:

	Original	Lowfat Version
Kcals. =	607	239
Chol. =	224 mg	35 mg
Sodium =	339 mg	357 mg
Fat =	54 grams	4 grams
Fat % =	82 %	14 %

Muffins and Breads

⌐

•

Basic Recipe Alteration Techniques
for Muffins and Breads

•

Biscuits and Muffins

•

Breakfast Breads

•

Miscellaneous Breads

Basic Recipe Alteration Techniques

•

Muffins and Breads

1. The oil in pancakes and waffles can be reduced by at least half when using a non-stick skillet or waffle maker. About one tablespoon of oil is sufficient.

2. Reduce sodium gradually in baked goods, ¼ teaspoon at a time. Since baking soda and baking powder contain sodium, the amount of salt in many baked goods can easily be reduced by half or more over time.

3. When reducing the amount of sugar in recipes, increase the amount of flavorings and spices up to twice as much.

4. Substitute lowfat margarine for regular margarine or shortening; use butter flavoring for baked goods that demand a buttery taste. Remember that margarine contains sodium, so omit all sodium in recipes in which you replace the shortening with diet margarine.

5. Most standard muffin recipes require less oil than called for. ¼ cup per 3 ½ to 4 cups of flour (or equivalent dry ingredients) is usually more than enough. If the recipe includes fruit or fruit juice, it will be plenty moist.

6. Yeast breads require little or no oil, about 1 tablespoon at most. Unless you are making a sweet bread, yeast dough will require some added sodium, about ⅛ to ¼ teaspoon will be adequate.

7. Never bake lowfat muffin batter in paper baking cups because they will stick to the paper. Use non-stick muffin tins or coat tins with vegetable cooking spray.

8. The texture of reduced fat breads and muffins is not quite as flaky but with less fat you can eat more without guilt! The best recipes include fruit in some form, ample spices or flavorings, and are tastiest when served warm. Store baked goods in the freezer, reheat in the microwave and do not overbake.

The following examples will demonstrate the above alteration techniques along with others. Remember that you can always spread jam or honey on a muffin you have altered if it does not seem sweet enough. Also, the easiest and tastiest muffins and breads you alter will be those that do not rely totally on fat and sugar for flavor and moisture.

Example #1 – Muffins and Breads

ANISE FLAVORED SCONES

Original Recipe:

½ cup currants or raisins
2 cups all-purpose flour
3 Tbls. brown sugar
2 tsp. baking powder
1 tsp. anise seed
½ tsp. baking soda
½ tsp. salt
⅓ cup butter
8 oz. sour cream
1 beaten egg yolk
1 beaten egg white
1 tsp. anise seed (optional)

Alterations:

*Use half white/half whole wheat

*Omit salt
* ⅓ cup diet margarine
*8 oz. plain or vanilla nonfat yogurt
* ⅛ cup Fleischmann's Egg Beaters

*Or add 1 tsp. anise flavoring

Directions:

COMBINE flours, brown sugar, baking powder, baking soda, and one teaspoon anise seed. Cut in diet margarine until mixture resembles coarse crumbs. Add currants or raisins and toss until mixed. Combine yogurt and *Egg Beaters* plus anise flavoring; add to flour mixture all at once. Using a fork, stir until just moistened.

TURN dough out onto a lightly floured surface. Quickly knead dough about 10 times; pat or roll dough into a 7 inch circle. Cut into 12 wedges and place on a non-stick baking sheet in a circle ½ inch apart. Brush scones with beaten egg white, and sprinkle with remaining anise seed, if desired. Bake at 400 for 10–12 minutes and serve warm. Makes 12 scones.

Nutritional Analysis:	Original	Lowfat Version
(per scone)		
Kcals. =	200	137
Chol. =	26 mg	0 mg
Sodium =	238 mg	175 mg
Fat =	10 grams	3 grams
Fat % =	45 %	18 %

Illustrated Alteration Technique Example #1:

1. Use half whole wheat (fine grind) flour to increase nutritional value and texture.
2. Omit added salt when recipes include lowfat margarine and baking powder/baking soda.
3. Substitute lowfat margarine for butter or regular margarine.
4. Use lowfat or nonfat yogurt when a recipe calls for sour cream.
5. If a recipe calls for an egg yolk, substitute with ⅛ cup *Fleischmann's Egg Beaters*.
6. Anise seed/flavoring is a powerful flavoring agent which makes it easy to reduce fat without compromising taste.
7. Sugar is not excessive in this recipe so it is not necessary to reduce it by half.

Example #2 – Muffins and Breads

BANANA NUT BREAD

Original Recipe:

1/3 cup shortening
1/2 cup sugar
2 eggs
1 3/4 cup flour

1 tsp. baking powder
1/2 tsp. baking soda
1/2 tsp. salt
1 cup mashed ripe bananas
1/2 cup chopped nuts

Alterations:

* 1/3 cup diet margarine
* 1/4 - 1/3 cup sugar
*4 egg whites
* 3/4 cup pastry whole wheat
   + 1 cup white

*Omit

* 1/4 cup nuts or omit

Directions:

CREAM together the diet margarine and sugar; add egg whites and beat well. Combine the flours, baking powder, and baking soda; add to creamed mixture alternately with the banana, blending well after each addition. Stir in nuts.

POUR into sprayed loaf pan and bake at 350 for about 40 minutes. Remove from pan and cool on a rack. Makes 12 servings.

Nutritional Analysis:	Original	Lowfat Version
Kcals. =	211	140
Chol. =	36 mg	0 mg
Sodium =	162 mg	141 mg
Fat =	10 grams	4 grams
Fat % =	41 %	27 %

Illustrated Alteration Technique Example #2:

1. Substitute lowfat margarine (6 grams of fat per tablespoon) for shortening.

2. Reduce sugar up to one half of original amount.

3. Substitute four egg whites for two whole eggs.

4. Use part whole wheat flour (fine grind–usually found in bulk sections of supermarkets). When flour amounts will be unequal, choose white flour for the larger quantity the first time you try the recipe.

5. Omit salt altogether due to presence of both diet margarine and baking powder/baking soda.

6. Bananas add a strong, sweet taste and plenty of moisture. Again, fat and sugar can easily be reduced without compromising flavor.

7. Always reduce the quantity of nuts. If you will not miss them or do not like them, omit entirely.

8. Diet margarine creamed with sugar does not look quite the same as regular margarine and sugar (will have a curdled appearance). This is not important, your product will turn out fine.

9. Any quick-bread recipe can also be prepared as muffins. Simply pour batter into nonstick muffin tins and bake at 400 for 20 minutes.

LITE BISCUITS

Original Recipe:

2 cups flour
1 Tbls. baking powder
½ tsp. salt
⅓ cup shortening
¾ cup milk

Alterations:

*Use at least ½ cup whole wheat flour

*Omit
* ⅓ cup diet margarine
* ¾ cup nonfat milk

Directions:

MIX flour and baking powder; cut in margarine until flour mixture is crumbly. Make a well in the center and add the milk all at once. Stir just until dough clings together. On a floured surface, knead dough 10 times. Pat dough down to ½ inch thickness. Cut with biscuit cutter. Place biscuits on a sprayed or non-stick cookie sheet. Bake at 450 for 10 - 12 minutes. Serve immediately. Makes 10 biscuits.

Nutritional Analysis:

	Original	Lowfat Version
Kcals. =	164	122
Chol. =	3 mg	0 mg
Sodium =	215 mg	181 mg
Fat =	8 grams	3 grams
Fat % =	42 %	24 %

CHOCOLATE CHIP SCONES

Original Recipe:

2 cups flour

3 Tbls. sugar
2 tsp. baking powder
¼ tsp. salt
½ cup diet margarine

½ cup nonfat milk
1 egg
1 tsp. vanilla
⅓ cup mini chocolate chips

Alterations:

*1 ½ cups white flour + ½ cup whole wheat pastry flour

*Optional
* ¼ cup diet margarine + ¼ cup nonfat yogurt or nonfat cream cheese

* ¼ cup Egg Beaters *or 2 egg whites*

Directions:

HEAT oven to 425 and spray baking sheet (or use non-stick). Combine flour, sugar, baking powder, and salt. Cut in diet margarine plus nonfat cream cheese (if using yogurt, wait and add it with the milk), until mixture resembles course crumbs. (DO NOT USE FOOD PROCESSOR).

In a small bowl combine the milk, egg substitute and vanilla (and yogurt if not using nonfat cream cheese). Add to dry ingredients along with chocolate chips and mix until mixture clings together and forms a soft dough (do this by hand). Turn out onto a lightly floured surface and knead 5 - 6 times. Roll to a 7-inch round and cut into 8 wedges. Sprinkle with a little sugar if desired and place scones about 1 inch apart on a baking sheet. Bake 15 minutes watching closely - should be very light brown on top. Makes 8 servings.

Nutritional Analysis:

	Original	Altered Version
Kcals. =	232	202
Chol. =	27 mg	0 mg
Sodium =	215 mg	157 mg
Fat =	9 grams	6 grams
Fat % =	34 %	25 %

BLUEBERRY MUFFINS

Original Recipe:

1 ¾ cups white flour

2 ½ tsps. baking powder
2 Tbls. sugar
¾ tsp. salt
1 egg
½ cup milk
¾ cup blueberries
⅓ cup oil

Alterations:

*1 cup whole wheat flour
* + ¾ cup white flour*

*2 Tbls. honey
*Omit salt
*2 egg whites or ¼ cup Egg Beaters

*2 Tbls. canola oil + 4 Tbls. apple juice
* concentrate*

Directions:

COMBINE dry ingredients. Make a well in the center. Beat egg whites and milk; add oil, honey, and apple juice concentrate to egg mixture. Stir wet and dry ingredients together and fold in the blueberries. Place batter evenly into non-stick or sprayed muffin tins. Makes 12 small or 6 Texas sized muffins. Bake at 400 for 20 minutes (if berries are frozen, you might need to bake them slightly longer).

Nutritional Analysis:

	Original	Lowfat Version
Kcals. =	292	225
Chol. =	38 mg	0 mg
Sodium =	426 mg	172 mg
Fat =	14 grams	5 grams
Fat % =	43 %	20 %

PINEAPPLE OATBRAN MUFFINS

Ingredients:

¼ cup canola oil
20 oz. crushed pineapple, undrained
2 cups pineapple juice made from concentrate
1 cup oatbran
2 cups old fashioned oats
½ cup brown sugar
1 ¾ cups whole wheat flour
1 ¾ cups white flour
¼ to ½ tsp. salt
2 tsps. vanilla + 1 tsp. coconut flavoring
2 ½ tsps. baking soda
1 tsp. baking powder
4 egg whites, slightly beaten
½ cup shredded coconut

Directions:

HEAT crushed pineapple and pineapple juice in a 4 cup glass pitcher or bowl in the microwave for about 4 minutes. Combine oatbran and oats in a large mixing bowl; add the hot fruit and juice; stir to combine and let stand for about 5 minutes. Add all remaining ingredients and mix well. Spoon into non-stick or sprayed large muffin tins. OPTIONAL: Sprinkle tops of muffins with a little shredded coconut. Bake at 400 for about 20 to 25 minutes. Makes 12 - 16 large Texas sized muffins.

Nutritional Analysis: (based on 12 muffins)

Kcals. =	347
Chol. =	0 mg
Sodium =	323 mg
Fat =	8 grams
Fat % =	19 %

PUMPKIN OR SWEET POTATO MUFFINS

Ingredients:

3 ½ cups whole wheat flour
1 ¾ cups white flour
2 ¼ tsps. baking soda
3 tsps. cinnamon
1 ½ tsps. ginger
1 ½ tsps. allspice
¾ tsp. baking powder
29 oz. canned pumpkin or mashed sweet potato
1 cup sugar
1 cup skim milk or fruit juice (1 ¼ - 1 ½ cups when using sweet potatoes)
⅓ cup vegetable or walnut oil
6 egg whites or ¾ cup Egg Beaters
Cinnamon and sugar mixture

Directions:

COMBINE all dry ingredients except sugar. Mix all wet ingredients together with the sugar. Add wet ingredients to dry and stir until moistened. Divide batter evenly among 16 Texas size non-stick muffin tins. Sprinkle each muffin with ½ tsp. cinnamon and sugar mixture. Bake at 400 for about 20 minutes or until a wooden toothpick inserted in center comes out clean. Remove from pan and let cool on a wire rack. Makes 16 large muffins. Serve with fruit spread or apple butter.

Nutritional Analysis:

Kcals. =	270
Chol. =	0 mg
Sodium =	164 mg
Fat =	5 grams
Fat % =	17 %

RHUBARB BREAD

Original Recipe:

1 1/2 cups brown sugar
1 egg
2/3 cup oil
1 tsp. vanilla
1 cup buttermilk
1 tsp. salt
2 1/2 cups flour
1 tsp. baking soda
1 tsp. cinnamon
1 cup walnuts, chopped
1 1/2 cups diced rhubarb

Alterations:

* 3/4 (or less) cup brown sugar
*2 egg whites
* 1/4 cup canola oil + 1/3 cup apple juice
*2 tsp. vanilla

*Omit
*Half whole wheat flour/half white

*Omit

Topping:

1/2 cup brown sugar
1 Tbls. melted butter

* 1/3 cup brown sugar
*Omit butter and add 1/3 cup chopped
   walnuts

Directions:

MIX all ingredients well, pour into two sprayed or non-stick loaf pans. Sprinkle with topping and bake at 325 for 45 - 60 minutes. Makes 20 servings.

Nutritional Analysis:	Original	Lowfat Version
Kcals. =	257	146
Chol. =	13 mg	0 mg
Sodium =	179 mg	70 mg
Fat =	12 grams	4 grams
Fat % =	41 %	26 %

PUMPKIN BREAD

Original Recipe:

1 cup sugar
1/2 cup brown sugar
1 cup cooked or canned pumpkin
1/2 cup cooking oil
2 eggs
2 cups flour
1 tsp. soda
1/2 tsp. each salt, nutmeg, cinnamon
1/4 tsp. ginger
1 cup raisins
1/2 cup chopped nuts
1/4 cup water

Alterations:

* 1/2 cup sugar
* 1/4 cup brown sugar

* 1/4 cup canola oil
*4 egg whites
*Half whole wheat/half white

*Omit salt or reduce to 1/4 tsp

* 1/4 cup chopped nuts
* 1/2 cup water

Directions:

COMBINE the sugars, pumpkin, oil, and egg whites; beat until well blended. Mix the flours, soda, and spices; add to the pumpkin mixture and stir well. Add raisins, nuts, and water. Spoon batter into a non-stick 9X5 loaf pan. Bake at 350 for 65 minutes or until done when tested. Wait about 10 minutes, remove bread from pan and cool on a wire rack. Makes 12 servings.

Nutritional Analysis:

	Original	Altered Version
Kcals. =	348	232
Chol. =	36	0 mg
Sodium =	176 mg	93 mg
Fat =	13 grams	7 grams
Fat % =	34 %	24 %

NOTE: Fat % can be reduced by omitting the nuts completely.

CRANBERRY ORANGE BREAD

Ingredients:

2 cups flour, half whole wheat
1/2 cup sugar
1 tsp. baking powder
1/2 tsp. salt
1/2 tsp. baking soda
1 cup cranberries, chopped
1/2 cup walnuts (optional)
1 tsp. shredded orange peel
2 egg whites
3/4 cup orange juice
1 Tbls. canola oil

Directions:

IN A LARGE BOWL, stir together dry ingredients; stir in cranberries, (walnuts) and orange peel. In a small bowl, combine egg whites, orange juice, and oil; add to the dry ingredients, stirring just until moistened. Bake in a sprayed or non-stick 8X4X2 inch loaf pan for 60 minutes at 350. Knife inserted in center should show slight moistness when withdrawn. Makes 10 servings.

Nutritional Analysis:	With Nuts	Without Nuts
Kcals. =	192	154
Chol. =	0	0
Sodium =	193 mg	193 mg
Fat =	5 grams	2 grams
Fat % =	25 %	10 %

ZUCCHINI CARROT BREAD

Original Recipe:

3 eggs
1 cup canola oil
1 ½ cups brown sugar
1 cup shredded zucchini
1 cup grated carrot
2 tsps. vanilla
2 ½ cups whole wheat flour
½ cup All-Bran *cereal*
1 tsp. salt
1 tsp. baking soda
3 tsp. cinnamon
1 cup chopped walnuts

Alterations:

*6 egg whites or ¾ cup Egg Beaters
* ¼ cup oil + ¾ cup apple juice
* ¾ cup brown sugar

*Or use Fiber One *cereal*
* ⅛ tsp. salt or omit

*Reduce to ½ cup or omit

Directions:

BEAT eggs whites, oil, and sugar. Add zucchini, carrot, and vanilla. Combine dry ingredients and add to wet ingredients. Pour into two non-stick or sprayed loaf pans and bake at 350 for about 60 minutes. Makes 20 servings.

Nutritional Analysis:

	Original	Lowfat Version
Kcals. =	268	144
Chol. =	32 mg	0 mg
Sodium =	187 mg	95 mg
Fat =	16 grams	5 grams
Fat % =	50 %	29 %

SPICED ZUCCHINI BREAD

Original Recipe:
1 cup grated zucchini
1 cup sugar
1/2 cup oil

2 eggs
1 1/2 cups flour
2 tsp. baking powder
1/2 tsp. soda, nutmeg, and ginger
1/2 tsp. salt
1 tsp. cinnamon
1/2 cup chopped walnuts

Alterations:

* 1/2 cup sugar
*2 Tbls. oil + 3/8 cup apple juice
    concentrate
*4 egg whites
*Use 1/2 cup whole wheat

*Reduce to 1/8 tsp. or omit

* 1/4 cup chopped nuts or omit

Directions:

MIX all ingredients thoroughly and pour into a non-stick or sprayed loaf pan. Bake at 350 for 45 to 55 minutes. Cool 15 minutes before removing from pan. Makes 10 servings.

Nutritional Analysis:

	Original	Lowfat Version
Kcals. =	300	179
Chol. =	43 mg	0 mg
Sodium =	228 mg	161 mg
Fat =	16 grams	5 grams
Fat % =	47 %	24 %

CARROT BANANA BREAD

Original Ingredients:	Alterations:
½ cup butter	** ¼ cup diet margarine*
1 cup brown sugar	** ½ cup brown sugar*
2 eggs	**4 egg whites*
1 cup mashed banana	**1 ¼ cup mashed banana*
2 cups white flour	**Half white/half whole wheat*
½ tsp. baking soda	
½ tsp. cinnamon	
¼ tsp. salt	**Omit salt*
1 cup shredded carrot	
½ cup chopped walnuts	** ¼ cup chopped walnuts or omit*

Directions:

CREAM margarine and sugar. Beat egg whites and mashed banana, and combine with sugar mixture. Mix all dry ingredients and add to wet ingredients. Stir in carrots and nuts. Pour batter into a non-stick loaf pan (9X5) and bake at 350 for 50 - 60 minutes. Cool completely. Serves 10.

Nutritional Analysis:	Original	Lowfat Version
Kcals. =	334	204
Chol. =	0 mg	0 mg
Sodium =	256 mg	185 mg
Fat =	14 grams	5 grams
Fat % =	38 %	19 %

BANANA NUT BREAD

Original:

¼ cup butter
1 ½ cup sugar
1 ½ cups mashed banana
2 eggs
1 tsp. vanilla
2 cups flour
2 tsp. baking powder
¾ tsp. salt
½ cup milk
¾ cup chopped nuts

Alterations:

* ¼ cup diet margarine
* ½ to ¾ cup sugar
*2 ¼ cups mashed banana
*4 egg whites or ½ cup Egg Beaters
*1 tsp. vanilla
*Half white/half whole wheat

*Omit
* ½ cup nonfat milk
*1 tsp. black walnut flavoring or use
⅛ cup walnut oil in place of
the diet margarine

Directions:

CREAM margarine and sugar; blend in mashed banana, egg substitute, and flavorings. Mix flour with baking powder and add to the banana mixture, stirring thoroughly. Pour batter into a non-stick loaf pan. Bake at 350 for about 1 hour. Serves 12.

Nutritional Analysis:

	Original	Lowfat Version
Kcals. =	300	185
Chol. =	47 mg	0 mg
Sodium =	238 mg	125 mg
Fat =	10 grams	2 grams
Fat % =	29 %	11 %

GRANDMA'S BANANA BREAD

Original Recipe:

½ cup shortening
1 cup sugar
2 eggs
½ cup chopped nuts
1 cup mashed banana
2 cups white flour
1 tsp. baking soda
½ tsp. salt

Alterations:

* ¼ cup diet margarine
* ½ cup sugar
*4 egg whites
* ¼ cup chopped nuts
*1 ¼ cups mashed banana
*Use half whole wheat flour

*Omit salt

Directions:

MIX all ingredients and pour into a non-stick loaf pan and bake at 350 for about 1 hour. Makes 8 generous slices.

Nutritional Analysis:	Original	Lowfat Version
Kcals. =	416	251
Chol. =	53 mg	0 mg
Sodium =	253 mg	200 mg
Fat =	19 grams	6 grams
Fat % =	41 %	20 %

BLUEBERRY COFFEECAKE

Original Recipe:

¾ cup sugar
⅓ cup flour
1 tsp. cinnamon
2 oz. margarine
2 ¼ cups sugar
2 eggs
¼ pound butter
3 ½ cups flour
1 cup milk
4 tsp. baking powder
1 tsp. salt
2 cups blueberries

Alterations:

* ½ cup sugar

*Use diet margarine
*1 cup sugar
*4 egg whites
* ¼ pound diet margarine (½ cup)
*Use half whole wheat or oat
*Use skim milk

* ¼ tsp. salt

Directions:

COMBINE first four ingredients until crumbly and set aside. Cream sugar and margarine; add egg whites and beat until light. Mix in milk. Stir dry ingredients together and add to liquid ingredients. Mix only until moistened. Stir in berries by hand. Spread in a 9X13 non-stick baking pan. Bake at 375 for about 45 minutes. For best flavor, serve warm. Serves 12.

Nutritional Analysis:	Original	Lowfat Version
Kcals. =	480	319
Chol. =	69 mg	0 mg
Sodium =	408 mg	322 mg
Fat =	8 grams	6 grams
Fat % =	25 %	17 %

CORNY BLUEBERRY COFFEECAKE

Ingredients:

1 ½ cups frozen blueberries
1 ½ cups white flour
1 ½ cups finely ground whole wheat flour
⅔ cup cornmeal
1 Tbls. baking powder
Pinch of salt
1 cup + 2 Tbls. nonfat yogurt
⅔ cup sugar
4 Tbls. sugar + 1 tsp. cinnamon, combined
8 Tbls. canola oil
1 Tbls. grated lemon peel
2 Tbls. lemon juice
½ cup Egg Beaters + 2 egg whites (or 6 egg whites)

Directions:

COMBINE flours, cornmeal, baking powder, and salt; set aside. Mix yogurt and lemon juice; set aside. Beat egg whites, *Egg Beaters*, ⅔ cup sugar, lemon peel, and oil; set aside. Add frozen blueberries to the flour mixture and toss to coat. Add all wet ingredients to the flour mixture, stirring gently until combined completely. Spread the stiff batter into a 9X13 non-stick pan. Sprinkle with remaining cinnamon and sugar mixture and bake at 375 for about 25 minutes or until center is firm to the touch. Serve warm for best flavor. 12 servings.

Nutritional Analysis:

Kcals. =	307
Chol. =	0 mg
Sodium =	152 mg
Fat =	10 grams
Fat % =	28 %

OATBRAN BUTTERMILK WAFFLES

Original Recipe:	Alterations:
1 cup oatbran	
1 cup whole wheat flour	
½ tsp. baking powder	
½ tsp. baking soda	
1 large egg	** ¼ cup Egg Beaters or 2 egg whites*
¼ cup salad oil	**2 Tbls. canola oil*
1 cup buttermilk	
1 cup milk	**Use nonfat milk*
Butter or margarine	**Use diet margarine*
Syrup	** ¼ cup low-sugar syrup per serving*

Directions:

IN A BOWL, stir together oatbran, flour, baking powder, and baking soda. Beat wet ingredients; egg substitute, oil, buttermilk, and nonfat milk. Add liquids to dry ingredients and stir until evenly moistened. Pour ⅓ batter in a preheated, non-stick waffle iron and bake until crisp and golden, about 4 to 5 minutes. Repeat with remaining batter. Serve each waffle with 1 teaspoon diet margarine and ¼ cup low-sugar syrup or warm fruit spread. Makes 3 waffles, 9-inch square (3 servings).

Nutritional Analysis:	Original	Lowfat Version
Kcals. =	760	627
Chol. =	95 mg	4 mg
Sodium =	411 mg	443 mg
Fat =	30 grams	15 grams
Fat % =	33 %	19 %

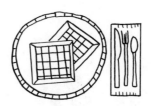

APPLE CORNYCAKE

Ingredients:

6 Tbls. lite pancake syrup
4 tsp. diet margarine, melted
2 large firm apples thinly sliced
¾ cup cornmeal
¾ cup whole wheat pastry flour
1 tsp. baking powder
½ tsp. baking soda
1 cup buttermilk (made from powdered)
2 egg whites or ¼ cup Egg Beaters
1 Tbls. canola oil

Directions:

PREHEAT oven to 375. Heat 2 Tbls. syrup and 1 teaspoon margarine in a non-stick saucepan over medium high heat; add sliced apples and saute for about 5 minutes or until slightly softened. Remove from heat and arrange slices decoratively in the bottom of a sprayed 10-inch quiche or casserole dish.

COMBINE the cornmeal, flour, baking powder, and baking soda. Beat the buttermilk, egg whites, and remaining ¼ cup syrup, melted margarine, and canola oil. Combine dry and wet ingredients, stirring just until combined. Spread batter over the apples and bake for 30 - 35 minutes. Cool slightly and invert on a serving platter. Cut into wedges and serve with additional warm lite syrup. Makes 8 servings.

Nutritional Analysis:

Kcals. =	406
Chol. =	2 mg
Sodium =	339 mg
Fat =	7 grams
Fat % =	15 %

BECKY'S BLUEBERRY CORNCAKES

Ingredients:

3 cups cornmeal
2 tsp. baking soda
1 ⅛ to 1 ¼ cup whole wheat flour
3 cups blueberries (fresh or frozen)
4 Tbls. honey
2 Tbls. canola oil
4 cups buttermilk (made from dry buttermilk powder)
4 egg whites

Directions:

COMBINE dry ingredients; combine wet ingredients and add to dry beating with an electric mixer. Fold in blueberries and let stand for about 10 minutes. Allow about ⅓ cup batter for each pancake. Cook until bubbly on a non-stick griddle; turn and cook until golden brown. Serves 6 - 8 (makes about 22 pancakes - 3 pancakes per person).

SERVE with reduced sugar maple syrup, light orange marmalade or powdered sugar. Yum!

Nutritional Analysis: (per pancake)

Kcals. =	145
Chol. =	2 mg
Sodium =	134 mg
Fat =	2 grams
Fat % =	13 %

TOMATO OAT BREAD

Original Recipe:
2 ½ cups white flour
1 Tbls. baking powder
1 tsp. salt
¼ cup sugar
1 cup oats
¼ cup + 2 Tbls. Parmesan cheese
1 Tbls. dried basil
1 tsp. thyme
2 eggs
1 cup milk
⅓ cup oil
2 tomatoes, peeled & chopped

Alterations:
*1 cup white/1 ½ cup whole wheat

*Omit salt
*Or reduce to 2 Tbls.

* ½ cup Egg Beaters
*1 ¼ cup nonfat milk
*2 Tbls. canola oil

Directions:

SPRAY a 9X5X3 inch loaf pan and line with waxed paper; spray paper also. Combine flour, baking powder, and sugar; add oats, ¼ cup Parmesan, basil, and thyme. Mix egg substitute with milk and oil; beat to combine completely. Combine wet and dry ingredients; fold in tomatoes. Pour into prepared pan and sprinkle top with remaining Parmesan. Bake in a preheated 375 oven for about 55 minutes. Cool for 10 minutes; loosen and turn out. Remove paper, turn right side up. Best served warm and sliced thickly. 8 servings.

Nutritional Analysis:

	Original	Lowfat Version
Kcals. =	350	276
Chol. =	60 mg	4 mg
Sodium =	495 mg	246 mg
Fat =	14 grams	6 grams
Fat % =	35 %	19 %

OAT BREAD

Original Recipe:

2 cups milk
½ cup margarine
½ cup honey
¼ cup sugar
2 cups oat bran
6 - 7 cups flour
2 packages yeast
½ cup water
3 egg whites
1 ½ tsp. salt

Alterations:

*Use skim milk
* ½ cup diet margarine

*Omit for a less sweet bread

*Use half whole wheat

* ½ tsp. salt or less

Directions:

SCALD milk, margarine, honey and sugar; cool. Combine oat bran and flour. Dissolve yeast in ½ cup warm water (add 1 teaspoon sugar to proof). Add proofed yeast and egg whites to milk mixture and beat to combine thoroughly. Add wet ingredients to the wheat flour and oat bran (this can be done in the food processor). Process until combined thoroughly. Pour batter into a large mixing bowl and add remaining white flour. Mix completely and knead; let rise until doubled. Punch down dough and divide for 3 - 4 small non-stick loaf pans. Let rise again until doubled and bake at 350 for 35 - 40 minutes. Makes 24 servings.

Nutritional Analysis:

	Original	Lowfat Version
Kcals. =	203	180
Chol. =	3 mg	0 mg
Sodium =	196 mg	109 mg
Fat =	5 grams	3 grams
Fat % =	22 %	13 %

POPPYSEED ROLLS

Original Recipe:
4 cups white flour
1 tsp. salt
2 Tbls. butter
1 egg
1 package dry yeast
1 tsp. sugar
½ cup milk + ½ cup hot water
1 beaten egg
Poppyseeds

Alterations:
*1 cup whole wheat/3 white
* ½ tsp. salt
*2 Tbls. diet margarine
* ¼ cup Egg Beaters *or 2 egg whites*

*Use skim milk + hot water
*Use 2 egg whites
*1 - 2 Tbls.

Directions:

COMBINE flours and salt in a food processor. Measure milk and hot water into a four cup glass measuring container; add margarine and sugar, warm for about 1 minute in the microwave. Add yeast to warm milk and let stand until mixture begins to foam. Add yeast mixture to flour and process for about 2 minutes (add a few extra tablespoons of white flour if dough is too sticky). Place dough into a sprayed plastic bowl and cover. Let rise until doubled. Punch dough down and shape into eight dough rounds. Place in a non-stick 9X13 pan evenly spaced and let rise in a warm place until doubled. Brush tops of rolls with beaten egg whites and sprinkle with poppy seeds. Bake at 375 for about 15 minutes. Makes 8 dinner rolls.

Nutritional Analysis:

	Original	Lowfat Version
Kcals. =	265	243
Chol. =	36 mg	0 mg
Sodium =	308 mg	191 mg
Fat =	5 grams	2 grams
Fat % =	18 %	10 %

Salads

—

•

Basic Recipe Alteration Techniques
for Salads

•

Salad Dressings

•

Side Salads

•

Side or Main Dish Salads

•

Fruit Salads

Basic Recipe Alteration Techniques
•
Salads

1. Substitute lowfat or nonfat mayonnaise and salad dressing in any recipe calling for regular mayonnaise or salad dressing. Again, use yogurt for sour cream.

2. Reduce the amount of oil when making packaged or homemade salad dressing; one to two tablespoons of vegetable or olive oil is plenty for an Italian type dressing and $1/2$ – 1 cup lite or nonfat mayonnaise is plenty for a creamy dressing (use nonfat yogurt for the remaining quantity).

3. Nonfat fruit flavored yogurt makes a great fruit salad dressing and *Quark* is a reasonable substitute for sour cream or cream cheese. Nonfat cream cheese and sour cream are also available at most grocery stores.

4. Lowfat pasta salad should be prepared without the dressing if made ahead; toss no sooner than 30 minutes before serving so increased water content of dressing will not soak into the pasta.

5. Fresh vegetable and fruit dips taste great made with nonfat yogurt or nonfat cream cheese.

6. Nonfat and lowfat bottled dressings are readily available and have improved significantly over the years; be willing to try a variety of brands until you find one you like.

7. When preparing tossed salads, include a wide variety of fresh vegetables to increase nutritional value (broccoli, cauliflower, green/red peppers, cucumbers, onions, mushrooms, cabbage, shredded carrot, tomatoes, zucchini).

8. Do not let high fat salad dressings (containing $1/2$ cup or more oil per recipe) intimidate you. Simply use 1–2 tablespoons of the oil and replace the remaining liquid with water. Put all ingredients in a small pan, add a little cornstarch and cook until slightly thickened. Cool until serving time. Voila! Lowfat dressing without all the sodium!

The following examples will illustrate healthier salad preparation techniques. Keep in mind that salads make wonderful main dishes during the warm weather months. They also can be prepared in advanced and stored in the refrigerator until serving time. If you want to serve leftovers the next day, let each individual toss their own serving with dressing.

Example #1 – Salads

24 HOUR LAYERED LETTUCE SALAD

Original Recipe:

1 head lettuce

½ cup sliced green onions
1 cup sliced celery
8 oz. sliced water chestnuts
10 oz. frozen peas, thawed
½ cup sliced radishes

Alterations:

*About 10 cups – use half romaine or leaf

LAYER the above ingredients in a 9X13 pan or large salad bowl, in the order given.

Dressing:

2 cups real mayonnaise
2 tsps. sugar
¾ cup grated Parmesan cheese
¾ tsp. seasoned salt
¾ tsp. garlic powder

*2 cups nonfat mayonnaise
*Omit

* ¾ tsp. Mrs. Dash's seasoning

MIX dressing ingredients well and spread on top of layered mixture. Cover and chill for 24 hours.

Condiments:

3 hard boiled eggs

¾ lb. bacon (crumbled)
2 tomatoes (chopped)

*1 hard boiled egg + 2 – 4 hard boiled whites
*4 oz. chopped lean turkey ham

BEFORE serving, sprinkle with the chopped egg and egg whites, chopped turkey ham, and tomatoes. Makes 8 servings.

Nutritional Analysis:

	Original	Lowfat Version
Kcals. =	768	165
Chol. =	154 mg	41 mg
Sodium =	1421 mg	408 mg
Fat =	69 grams	4 grams
Fat % =	80 %	23 %

Illustrated Alteration Technique Example #1:

1. Use a mixture of greens for more nutritional value.

2. Substitute lowfat or nonfat mayonnaise for regular mayonnaise. You could also use half lowfat and half nonfat mayonnaise.

3. Use no-salt seasonings. There is plenty of salt in the Parmesan cheese and it is a more important flavoring agent for maintaining good taste when fat is reduced.

4. Always reduce egg yolks or eliminate them whenever possible; each yolk contains six grams of fat and about 214 mg cholesterol.

5. Never use bacon; it is almost 100 % fat and highly saturated. Bacon flavor is easily duplicated by using small amounts of lean turkey ham or Canadian bacon.

Example #2 – Salads

FRENCH DRESSING

Original Recipe:
½ cup sugar
½ cup vinegar
½ cup catsup
½ cup canola oil
1 tsp. Worcestershire
¼ tsp. salt
½ cup minced onions

Alterations:
* ¼ - ⅓ cup sugar

*2 Tbls. canola oil + ⅓ cup water
*1 tsp. lite Worcestershire
*Omit salt

*2 - 3 tsps. cornstarch

Directions:

SIMMER all ingredients until slightly thickened. Chill thoroughly. Makes 19 servings (1 ounce = 2 tablespoons).

Nutritional Analysis:	Original	Lowfat Version
Kcals. =	80	43
Chol. =	0 mg	0 mg
Sodium =	123 mg	95 mg
Fat =	6 grams	1.5 grams
Fat % =	62 %	29 %

Illustrated Alteration Technique Example #2:

1. This dressing is quite sweet with ½ cup sugar; be conservative with your first reduction though.

2. Reduce fat to 1 – 2 tablespoons and replace remaining liquid quantity with water.

3. Always use low sodium products when available.

4. Omit added salt; there is plenty in the catsup and lite Worcestershire sauce.

5. Use cornstarch to thicken dressing over stove. If the dressing seems too thick, add a little more water.

POPPYSEED DRESSING

Original Recipe:

1 ½ cups sugar
2 tsps. dry mustard
2 tsps. salt
⅔ cup vinegar
3 Tbls. onion juice (about ⅔ medium
    onion, pureed)
2 cups salad oil

4 Tbls. poppyseeds

Alterations:

* ½ to ¾ cup sugar

* ¼ tsp. salt or omit

*2 Tbls. canola oil + 2 cups water +
    2 - 3 Tbls. cornstarch

Directions:

COMBINE all ingredients in a small saucepan and cook until smooth and thickened. Chill until serving time. Makes 48 servings (1 ¾ tablespoons each serving).

Nutritional Analysis:	Original	Lowfat Version
Kcals. =	110	24
Chol. =	0 mg	0 mg
Sodium =	92 mg	15 mg
Fat =	9 grams	1 gram
Fat % =	75 %	33 %

ROQUEFORT DRESSING

Original Recipe:
1 pint mayonnaise
1 pint sour cream
6 oz. Roquefort cheese
2 Tbls. vinegar
1 tsp. mustard
Salt and garlic to taste

Alterations:
*16 oz. fat-free mayonnaise
*16 oz. nonfat yogurt
*3 oz. Roquefort or Blue cheese

*Omit salt

Directions:

COMBINE all ingredients and store in the refrigerator. Makes 40 servings (1 ounce or 2 tablespoons per serving).

Nutritional Analysis:

	Original	Lowfat Version
Kcals. =	121	18
Chol. =	15 mg	2 mg
Sodium =	158 mg	46 mg
Fat =	13 grams	1 gram
Fat % =	92 %	33 %

SPINACH SALAD DRESSING

Original Recipe:
½ medium onion
⅓ cup cider vinegar
⅓ cup sugar
1 tsp. dry mustard
1 tsp. salt
¾ Tbls. poppyseeds
1 cup oil

Alterations:
*Puree or chop finely

*Omit salt

*1 Tbls. canola oil or olive oil
*1 cup water + ½ Tbls. cornstarch

Directions:

COMBINE sugar, cornstarch, dry mustard, and poppyseeds; add cold water, stirring to combine. Add vinegar, oil, and pureed onion; heat until boiling and dressing thickens slightly. Cool and pour into a glass jar or salad dressing container. Chill. Serves 16 (1 ounce or 2 tablespoons per person).

Nutritional Analysis:	Original	Lowfat Version
Kcals. =	141	29
Chol. =	0 mg	0 mg
Sodium =	138 mg	5 mg
Fat =	14 grams	1 gram
Fat % =	86 %	31 %

THREE BEAN
SALAD

Original Recipe:

1 can green beans
1 can yellow wax beans, drained
1 can red kidney beans, drained
1/2 cup minced green peppers
1/2 cup minced onion
1/2 cup salad oil

1/2 cup vinegar
3/4 cup sugar
1 tsp. salt
1/2 tsp. pepper

Alterations:

*16 oz. frozen green beans, cooked

*Rinse to remove excess sodium

*2 Tbls. canola oil + 1/2 cup water +
   2 tsps. cornstarch

* 1/3 - 1/2 cup sugar
*Omit

Directions:

THE day before serving, drain and rinse canned beans, cook frozen green beans and place all in a bowl with the green peppers and onion. Combine canola oil, water, vinegar, cornstarch, sugar, and pepper in a small saucepan; cook until smooth and thickened. Toss beans with dressing and chill until serving time. Serves 6 - 8.

Nutritional Analysis:

	Original	Lowfat Version
Kcals. =	361	190
Chol. =	0 mg	0 mg
Sodium =	502 mg	147 mg
Fat =	19 grams	5 grams
Fat % =	44 %	22 %

COLESLAW

Original Recipe:

1 cup vinegar
½ cup canola oil
1 tsp. dry mustard
¼ tsp. salt
1 tsp. celery seed
1 cabbage, finely shredded (8 - 10 cups)
¾ cup sugar
1 onion, minced
1 red pepper, chopped

Alterations:

* ¼ cup oil + ¼ cup water or juice

*Optional

*Reduce to ½ cup

Directions:

SHRED cabbage and mince onion; sprinkle with sugar and set aside. In a small saucepan, combine the first five ingredients and bring to a boil. Pour over cabbage and mix thoroughly. Add chopped red pepper and mix again. Let sit for at least ½ hour. Transfer to a smaller container and refrigerate overnight. Lasts for a week. Serves 10 to 12.

Nutritional Analysis:

	Original	Lowfat Version
Kcals. =	182	134
Chol. =	0 mg	0 mg
Sodium =	73 mg	73 mg
Fat =	11 grams	6 grams
Fat % =	52 %	36 %

LINGUINI SALAD

Original Recipe:

1 lb. Linguini pasta, cooked
2 tomatoes, chopped finely
1 cucumber or zucchini, chopped
1 onion, minced
Your favorite Mrs. Dash's *spices*
Nonfat or lowfat bottled Italian salad dressing (about ¾ to 1 cup)

Directions:

COMBINE pasta and vegetables; season and toss with salad dressing right before serving. Makes 4 servings.

NOTE: This type of salad can easily become a main dish by adding a bag of slightly cooked mixed vegetables (broccoli, cauliflower, carrot) and some type of protein (kidney beans, shrimp, or chicken pieces). Served with whole wheat rolls and a fresh fruit salad, it is a complete meal in minutes!

Nutritional Analysis:

Kcals. =	491
Chol. =	2 mg
Sodium =	785 mg (sodium will be less if you make your own dressing)
Fat =	2 grams
Fat % =	3 %

PICNIC POTATO SALAD

Original Recipe:

5 potatoes, cooked
5 eggs, hard boiled
2 dill pickles, chopped
½ onion chopped
1 tsp. yellow mustard
¼ tsp. pepper
1 Tbls. catsup
2 Tbls. Thousand Island dressing
½ cup mayonnaise

Alterations:

*Remove 2 yolks

*Use low-sodium if available
*Use lowfat or nonfat dressing
* ½ cup nonfat salad dressing or
  mayonnaise

Directions:

COMBINE all ingredients and chill. Serves 6.

Nutritional Analysis:

	Original	Lowfat Version
Kcals. =	229	176
Chol. =	183 mg	107 mg
Sodium =	526 mg	448 mg
Fat =	9 grams	3 grams
Fat % =	34 %	17 %

CHICKEN SALAD
HONOLULU

Original Recipe:

1 lb. skinless chicken breast meat
⅔ cup instant rice
1 cup diced celery
13 oz. pineapple tidbits, drained
1 small can mandarin oranges
1 cup mayonnaise
1 Tbls. lemon juice
1 tsp. grated onion
1 tsp. salt
¼ tsp. pepper

Alterations:

*1 cup nonfat mayonnaise

*Omit and add a no-salt seasoning blend

Directions:

COOK chicken until tender and dice. Bring ⅔ cup water to boil. Add the rice and moisten well. Cover and remove from heat; let stand 5 minutes. Uncover and cool. Mix rice, chicken, celery, pineapple, and oranges together; chill. Combine fat-free mayonnaise, lemon juice, onion, and seasonings; stir dressing into rice just before serving. Serve on lettuce. Makes 6 servings.

Nutritional Analysis:

	Original	Lowfat Version
Kcals. =	442	200
Chol. =	65 mg	44 mg
Sodium =	635 mg	270 mg
Fat =	30 grams	2 grams
Fat % =	61 %	6 %

CHINESE CABBAGE SALAD

Original Recipe:

2 packages of Top Ramen *noodles*
4 green onions, chopped
4 cups diced chicken
2 oz. slivered almonds
1 head shredded purple or green cabbage
1 cup shredded carrots
½ cup mayonnaise
½ cup soy sauce

1 cup water chestnuts
½ tsp. garlic powder
½ tsp. salt
¼ tsp. pepper

Alterations:

*Use chicken breast meat
*Optional or reduce to 1 oz.
*About 8 cups

* ½ cup nonfat mayonnaise
* ⅛ cup low-sodium soy sauce + ⅛ cup
    rice vinegar

*Omit salt

Directions:

COOK noodles and place in a bowl (discard seasoning packet). Add all remaining ingredients and toss well. Can be served hot as a main dish or cold as a salad. Serves 8.

Nutritional Analysis:	Original	Lowfat Version
Kcals. =	340	212
Chol. =	71 mg	59 mg
Sodium =	1387 mg	465 mg
Fat =	21 grams	6 grams
Fat % =	54 %	25 %

PASTA AND SHRIMP SALAD

Original Recipe:

12 oz. shell pasta, cooked
10 oz. frozen peas, thawed
1 ½ cups chopped celery
3 oz. cubed cheddar cheese
½ lb. small shrimp, cooked
12 chopped olives
2 chopped green onions
½ cup mayonnaise
½ cup sour cream
1 ½ tsps. mustard
Dash of salt
Dash of pepper

Alterations:

*Use lowfat cheddar cheese

* ½ cup pickle relish

*Use nonfat mayonnaise
*Use low or nonfat yogurt or Quark

*Omit

*Optional: pimento for color, water
chestnuts, other vegetables

Directions:

TOSS all of the above ingredients and chill for no longer than 30 minutes. Serves 8 - 10.
If prepared in advance, toss right before serving.

Nutritional Analysis:

	Original	Lowfat Version
Kcals. =	406	229
Chol. =	75 mg	60 mg
Sodium =	360 mg	351 mg
Fat =	20 grams	7 grams
Fat % =	43 %	20 %

LINGUINI SALAD ELEGANCE

Original Recipe:
8 oz. dry Linguini, cooked
8 oz. Zesty Italian dressing
1 cucumber, cut-up
1 onion, chopped
1 green pepper, chopped
½ bottle Salad Elegance (1 oz.)

12 oz. sliced ripe olives

Alterations:
*12 oz. Linguini, cooked
*Use Lite Zesty Italian dressing

*Half green pepper, half red pepper
*2 Tbls. toasted sesame seeds, 2 oz. grated Parmesan cheese, 1 tsp. Mrs. Dash seasoning (a light version of Salad Elegance is available)
*Omit olives; add 16 oz. slightly cooked California Mix frozen vegetables

Directions:
COMBINE all ingredients and toss with dressing no more than 30 minutes before serving. Make 4 main dish servings or 8 side dish servings.

Nutritional Analysis:

	Original	Lowfat Version
Kcals. =	499	508
Chol. =	14 mg	14 mg
Sodium =	1991 mg	739 mg
Fat =	24 grams	14 grams
Fat % =	41 %	24 %

FRESH BROCCOLI
SALAD

Original Recipe:

4 cups chopped fresh broccoli
½ cup chopped red onion
½ cup dry sunflower seeds
1 lb. crisp bacon
½ cup mayonnaise
¼ cup sugar
2 Tbls. vinegar

Alterations:

*8 cups chopped broccoli

* ¼ cup sunflower seeds, toasted
*2 slices chopped cooked Canadian bacon
*1 cup nonfat mayonnaise
*1 - 2 Tbls. sugar
*2 - 4 Tbls. vinegar

Directions:

COMBINE mayonnaise, sugar, and vinegar; set aside. Mix remaining ingredients and chill. Just before serving, toss broccoli mixture with dressing. 6 - 8 servings.

Nutritional Analysis:

	Original	Lowfat Version
Kcals. =	681	121
Chol. =	75 mg	5 mg
Sodium =	1327 mg	195 mg
Fat =	57 grams	4 grams
Fat % =	75 %	26 %

FETA TORTELLINI SALAD

Original Recipe:

2 9-oz. packages fresh Tortellini

2 red and green peppers, cut into
    thin strips
1 small red onion, thinly sliced
¼ cup sliced pitted ripe olives

Dressing:

½ cup rice wine vinegar
½ cup olive oil

3 Tbls. dried mint (optional)
3 Tbls. lemon juice
2 Tbls. dry sherry

1 ½ tsps. seasoned salt
1 tsp. garlic powder
⅛ tsp. crushed red pepper
¼ tsp. black pepper
½ cup crumbled Feta cheese

Alterations:

*16 oz. dry Tortellini, cooked and
    drained

*Omit

*2 Tbls. olive oil + ⅓ cup water +
    2 - 3 tsps. cornstarch

*Or use 2 Tbls. apple juice + ½ tsp.
    sherry flavoring
*2 tsps. Mrs. Dash's seasoning blend

Directions:

COMBINE cooked pasta, peppers, and onion; chill. For dressing, combine vinegar, oil, water, cornstarch, mint, lemon juice, sherry, seasonings, garlic powder, red pepper, and black pepper; cook until thickened and chill. Pour dressing over salad about 30 minutes before serving. Stir in cheese. Makes 12 servings.

Nutritional Analysis:

	Original	Lowfat Version
Kcals. =	236	152
Chol. =	27 mg	12 mg
Sodium =	415 mg	230 mg
Fat =	13 grams	7 grams
Fat % =	57 %	39 %

TORTELLINI ROMAINE SALAD

Ingredients:

9 oz. Tortellini pasta, cooked
2 oz. fresh Parmesan cheese, shredded
1 cup cooked (but crisp) asparagus
½ cup cooked carrots
12 cups torn romaine lettuce pieces
3 Tbls. lemon juice
2 Tbls. water
1 ½ Tbls. olive oil
1 tsp. dried basil
1 clove minced garlic
⅛ tsp. black pepper

Directions:

COMBINE dressing ingredients; lemon juice, water, olive oil, basil, garlic, and pepper. Store in the refrigerator until time to serve salad. Combine cooked pasta, romaine, asparagus, and carrots. Chill until serving time. Right before serving, toss salad with fresh Parmesan and dressing. Serve with hot whole grain bread. Serves 6. Fresh strawberries and nonfat frozen yogurt completes this wonderful summer meal.

Nutritional Analysis:

Kcals. =	269
Chol. =	9 mg
Sodium =	227 mg
Fat =	8 grams
Fat % =	26 %

NOTE: *Cooking Light Magazine* is still the best source for healthy recipes and sound exercise information.

ADAPTED FROM COOKING LIGHT MAGAZINE

HOT POTATO SALAD

Original Recipe: Alterations:

10 new potatoes, cut into chunks
3 carrots sliced in rounds
2 cups broccoli flowerets
1 cup fresh green beans (one inch pieces)
8 oz. kielbasa sausage, cut in rounds   **2 slices chopped Canadian bacon*
½ cup grated Parmesan cheese   ** ¼ cup Parmesan*

Vinaigrette Dressing:

¼ cup balsamic vinegar
1 Tbls. lemon juice
1 tsp. Dijon mustard
1 clove garlic, minced
1 Tbls. chopped parsley
½ tsp. each thyme, dill, marjoram,
*   basil, oregano*
½ cup olive oil   **1 Tbls. olive oil + ⅓ cup water and*
                                                   *   ½ Tbls. cornstarch + 2 Tbls. sugar*

Directions:

STEAM or microwave all vegetables until just tender. Brown the Canadian bacon pieces and add to the vegetables. Combine all dressing ingredients and cook in a non-stick pan until thickened. Toss hot vegetables with warm dressing and sprinkle with the Parmesan cheese. Serve immediately. 8 servings.

Nutritional Analysis:	Original	Lowfat Version
Kcals. =	284	93
Chol. =	23 mg	5 mg
Sodium =	513 mg	251 mg
Fat =	23 grams	3 grams
Fat % =	71 %	30 %

CREAMY COTTAGE
CHEESE SALAD

Original Ingredients:

1 small package lime Jello
1 cup boiling water
1 cup fine curd cottage cheese
1 cup undrained crushed pineapple
1 cup cream, whipped

12 marshmallows, coarsely cut
¼ cup chopped walnuts

Alterations:

*Use sugar-free lime Jello

*Use 1% lowfat or nonfat cottage cheese

*1 cup prepared Dream Whip *(made
    with nonfat milk)*
*6 marshmallows
*2 Tbls. chopped walnuts

Directions:

DISSOLVE the *Jello* in boiling water and let set partially. Add the cottage cheese and crushed pineapple. Combine with a mixer and let set in the refrigerator for about one hour. Add the prepared *Dream Whip*, marshmallows and nuts; beat with mixer. Place in refrigerator until ready to serve. Serves 8.

Nutritional Analysis:

	Original	Lowfat Version
Kcals. =	250	88
Chol. =	45 mg	1 mg
Sodium =	129 mg	129 mg
Fat =	15 grams	3 grams
Fat % =	51 %	24 %

LEMON JELLO
SALAD

Original Recipe:

1 large package lemon Jello *(6 oz.)*

⅓ cup sugar
1 Tbls. lemon juice
1 cup drained crushed pineapple
1 cup Cool Whip

1 cup grated cheddar cheese
½ cup chopped nuts

Alterations:

**Use sugar-free Jello to reduce
   kcalories further*
*Reduce or omit sugar

**1 cup Dream Whip prepared with
   nonfat milk*
*Use lowfat cheddar cheese
* ¼ cup chopped nuts (optional)

Directions:

DISSOLVE *Jello* in 1 cup boiling water. Add lemon juice; cool and let set partially. Beat until frothy and light. Fold in pineapple, prepared *Dream Whip*, grated cheese, and nuts. Serves 8.

Nutritional Analysis:

	Original	Lowfat Version
Kcals. =	282	235
Chol. =	16 mg	10 mg
Sodium =	103 mg	73 mg
Fat =	11 grams	6 grams
Fat % =	33 %	23 %

24- HOUR FRUIT SALAD

Original Recipe:

1 pint sour cream
16 oz. mandarin oranges
12 oz. maraschino cherries
16 oz. crushed pineapple, drained
2 cups miniature marshmallows
1 cup shredded coconut

Alterations:

*16 oz. lowfat plain yogurt

*16 oz. sweet cherries

Directions:

COMBINE all ingredients and chill overnight.

Nutritional Analysis:

	Original	Lowfat Version
Kcals. =	335	249
Chol. =	25 mg	4 mg
Sodium =	80 mg	89 mg
Fat =	16 grams	5 grams
Fat % =	41 %	18 %

Desserts

•

Basic Recipe Alteration Techniques
for Desserts

•

Cookies

•

Cakes

•

Pies and Pastries

•

Puddings

•

Candy

Basic Recipe Alteration Techniques

•

Desserts

1. Most lowfat cookies will have a moist and chewy rather than a crispy texture. Also, since they do not spread as much, remember to shape and flatten them prior to baking.

2. Choose cookie recipes that rely on fruits and fruit juices instead of sugar and butter to supply most of the sweetening and moisture. Applesauce and other pureed fruits can be substituted for most of the oil or butter in cake and cookie recipes.

3. Instead of spreading a thick layer of frosting on cakes, glaze cakes while warm with a thin powdered sugar frosting.

4. When preparing lowfat pie crust, handle the dough as little as possible or press the dough into the sprayed pie plate with a fork or fingers. Lowfat pie crust should always contain some whole grain flour for texture; it helps make the pastry flaky without fat.

5. For fruit pie fillings, use concentrated fruit juices plus cornstarch to thicken and sweeten. Added butter or margarine is not necessary. Use a little butter flavoring if desired.

6. Evaporated skim milk can be substituted for cream or regular evaporated milk in all custard pies such as pumpkin. Prepare *Dream Whip* with skim milk for a lowfat whipped cream topping.

7. Lowfat margarine does not melt like regular margarine due to the higher water content. Although it looks different and results in a slightly altered product texture, lowfat margarine works well in most recipes. ALWAYS use lowfat margarine that contains six grams of fat per tablespoon.

8. When a recipe calls for oat flour, it can be purchased or made quite easily by grinding raw oats in a food processor.

The following examples will illustrate thoroughly tested techniques for reducing fat and sugar in your favorite desserts. Please keep in mind that, unlike my first cookbook, Nutritious and Delicious II contains more desserts that do not have a high nutritional value. However, as long as those desserts are consumed infrequently (such as the lowfat fudge), it has been my experience that it is very important not to feel deprived of "once-in-a-while" favorites.

Example #1 – Desserts

EASY SUGAR COOKIES

Original Recipe:

4 eggs
4 cups sugar
1 cup butter
2 cups canned milk
1 ½ tsps. vanilla
6 tsps. baking powder
Dash of salt
8 cups flour

Alterations:

*1 cup Egg Beaters
*2 cups sugar
*1 cup diet margarine
*Use evaporated skim milk
*2 tsps. vanilla + 1 tsp. butter flavoring

*Half whole wheat + 2 tsps. nutmeg

Directions:

CREAM margarine and sugar; beat in egg substitute, vanilla, butter flavoring, and evaporated skim milk. Mix flours, salt, and nutmeg and stir into wet ingredients. Drop onto a sprayed or non-stick cookie sheet. Dip a small glass into a mixture of cinnamon and sugar and flatten each cookie (dipping glass into sugar for each cookie). Bake at 350 for 12 minutes. Makes 70 cookies.

Nutritional Analysis:	Original	Lowfat Version
Kcals. =	119	78
Chol. =	21 mg	0 mg
Sodium =	68 mg	82 mg
Fat =	4 grams	1 gram
Fat % =	27 %	16 %

Illustrated Alteration Technique Example #1:

1. Substitute *Egg Beaters* for the whole eggs.

2. Reduce sugar by half.

3. Use diet margarine (6 grams of fat per tablespoon) in place of butter. Add butter flavoring if desired.

4. Increase flavorings when reducing fat, especially when the recipe relies on fat and sugar for most of its flavor. This revision has more vanilla than the original recipe and also adds butter flavoring and nutmeg for a more interesting taste.

5. This cookie will have a softer texture compared to the original due to the reduction in fat.

Example #2 – Desserts

APPLE CAKE

Original Recipe:

4 cups diced apples
2 cups sugar
2 eggs
1/2 cup canola oil
1 cup chopped walnuts
1 cup raisins
2 tsps. vanilla
2 tsps. cinnamon
2 cups white flour
2 tsp. baking soda
1 tsp. salt

Alterations:

*1 cup sugar
* 1/2 cup Egg Beaters
* 1/4 cup canola oil + 1/4 cup apple juice
* 1/2 cup chopped walnuts
*Plump raisins before adding to batter

*Use half whole wheat pastry flour

*Omit

Glaze:

3 cups powdered sugar
1/2 cup margarine
1 tsp. vanilla
3 to 4 Tbls. hot water

*1 cup powdered sugar
* 1/4 tsp. butter flavoring

*1 Tbls. evaporated skim milk or nonfat
    cream cheese

Directions:

COMBINE all of the cake ingredients and spread into a non-stick 9X13 pan. Bake at 350 for about 40 minutes or until cake has shrunk from the sides of the pan. If you use a glass baking pan, reduce heat to 325. Glaze cake with a thin mixture of one cup powdered sugar, butter flavoring, vanilla, and evaporated skim milk. Frost and serve warm. Makes 12 servings.

Nutritional Analysis:	Original	Lowfat Version
Kcals. =	589	316
Chol. =	35 mg	0 mg
Sodium =	418 mg	159 mg
Fat =	24 grams	8 grams
Fat % =	36 %	22 %

Illustrated Alteration Technique Example #2:

1. Choosing recipes with fresh fruit makes it easier to produce a tasty product when reducing fat and sugar.

2. Reduce sugar by half.

3. Substitute ¼ cup *Egg Beaters* or 2 egg whites for every whole egg.

4. Reduce oil by half and replace the missing liquid quantity with a complementary fruit juice.

5. Always reduce or omit nuts.

6. Plump dried fruits (cover with hot water, soak briefly, and drain) before adding to lowfat baked goods. It will prevent them from drawing moisture from the batter.

7. Use half whole wheat flour for better texture and more nutritional value.

8. Omit salt, especially whenever baking soda and/or baking powder are present.

9. Glaze lightly rather than use fatty frostings. Totally nonfat frosting is easy to make with evaporated skim milk or nonfat cream cheese. Frosting should be made thicker than usual and applied to cakes when warm. This technique is illustrated several times in the dessert section of this cookbook.

SUPER DUPER OATMEAL COOKIES

Original Recipe:

1 cup white sugar
16 oz. brown sugar
6 eggs
1 cup peanut butter
6 cups rolled oats
2 cups white flour
1 cup chopped nuts
1 cup chocolate chips
1 cup raisins
1 tsp. salt
1 tsp. baking soda
1 tsp. baking powder
1 tsp. vanilla
1 cup shortening

Alterations:

* ½ cup white sugar
*1 cup brown sugar
* 1 ½ cup Egg Beaters
* ½ cup peanut butter

*2 cups whole wheat flour
* ½ cup nuts or omit
*Or butterscotch chips

*Omit salt - add 2 tsps. cinnamon

*2 - 3 tsps. vanilla
* ½ cup diet margarine + 1 cup
*   nonfat yogurt or cream cheese*

Directions:

CREAM diet margarine, sugars, and peanut butter; add yogurt, egg substitute, and vanilla, mixing until smooth. Combine flour, oats, soda, baking powder, and cinnamon; add to wet ingredients and stir thoroughly. Add raisins (plump first), and chocolate chips (nuts are optional). Drop by rounded teaspoonfuls and bake on non-stick cookie sheets for about 12 - 15 minutes at 350. About 60 cookies

Nutritional Analysis:

	Original	Lowfat Version (with nuts)	(without nuts)
Kcals. =	186	127	121
Chol. =	21 mg	0 mg	0 mg
Sodium =	86 mg	65 mg	64 mg
Fat =	9 grams	5 grams	4 grams
Fat % =	41 %	32 %	29 %

FAT-FREE OATMEAL COOKIES

Original Recipe:

1 cup flour
1 cup oats
½ cup sugar
½ tsp. salt (omit or reduce)
½ tsp. baking powder
½ tsp. baking soda
½ tsp. cinnamon
⅓ cup light Karo syrup
2 egg whites
1 tsp. vanilla
½ cup raisins (plumped)

Directions:

PREHEAT oven to 375. Spray cookie sheets. In a large bowl combine dry ingredients. Stir in egg whites, corn syrup, and vanilla until well mixed. Add raisins. Drop by rounded teaspoonfuls. Bake for about 10 minutes. Makes 2 dozen cookies.

Nutritional Analysis:

Kcals. =	72
Chol. =	0 mg
Sodium =	76 mg
Fat =	0 grams
Fat % =	3 %

SUNFLOWER SEED COOKIES

Original Recipe:

2 cups flour
2 ½ tsps. baking powder
1 ½ tsps. cinnamon
½ tsp. salt
½ tsp. baking soda
¼ tsp. cloves
½ cup butter
½ cup sugar
1 egg
⅓ cup orange juice concentrate, thawed
½ cup honey
1 cup raisins
1 cup oats
½ cup sunflower seeds

Alterations:

*1 cup white/1 cup whole wheat

*Omit

* ½ cup diet margarine
* ¼ cup sugar
*2 egg whites
*Plus 2 tsps. grated orange peel

*Plump raisins

* ⅓ cup sunflower seeds

Directions:

MIX dry ingredients. Cream margarine and sugar; add egg whites. Add dry ingredients to creamed mixture alternately with the honey and orange juice concentrate. Stir in oats, raisins, sunflower seeds, and orange peel. Drop onto a non-stick cookie sheet and bake at 350 for 15 to 20 minutes. Makes about 36 cookies.

Nutritional Analysis:

	Original	Lowfat Version
Kcals. =	118	96
Chol. =	13 mg	0 mg
Sodium =	92 mg	72 mg
Fat =	4 grams	2 grams
Fat % =	31 %	21 %

COWBOY COOKIES

Original Recipe:

2 cups margarine

2 cups white sugar
2 cups brown sugar
4 eggs

2 tsps. baking powder
2 tsps. baking soda
4 cups flour

Alterations:

*1 cup diet margarine + 1 cup nonfat
    cream cheese

*1 cup white sugar
*1 cup brown sugar
*4 egg whites + ½ cup skim milk +
    2 tsps. vanilla

*2 white/2 whole wheat

Directions:

CREAM margarine, nonfat cream cheese, and sugars; beat in egg whites, vanilla, and milk. Add dry ingredients; mix well.

ADD the following:

2 cups coconut
2 cups chopped nuts
2 cups butterscotch chips
4 cups rolled oats
4 cups crushed corn flakes

*1 cup coconut
*1 cup nuts (optional)
*1 cup chocolate chips

If batter feels too stiff, add an additional ½ cup nonfat milk. Bake at 350 for 12 minutes. Makes 72 (2 - 3 inch) cookies.

Nutritional Analysis:

	Original	Lowfat Version	Without Nuts
Kcals. =	204	117	104
Chol. =	12 mg	0 mg	0
Sodium =	131 mg	100 mg	99
Fat =	10 grams	4 grams	3
Fat % =	44 %	30 %	23 %

OATMEAL RAISIN COOKIES

Original Recipe:

1 cup white flour
3/4 tsp. baking soda
1/2 tsp. salt
1/2 tsp. nutmeg
1 tsp. cinnamon
1 1/2 cups brown sugar
1 tsp. vanilla
2 eggs
3/4 cup canola oil

1 cup raisins
2 cups oats

Alterations:

*Use half wheat

*Omit or use less

* 1/2 to 3/4 cup brown sugar

*4 egg whites or 1/2 cup Egg Beaters
* 1/4 cup canola oil + 1/2 cup apple juice
  concentrate
*Plump raisins before adding

Directions:

COMBINE flours, soda, nutmeg, and cinnamon. Add oil, juice concentrate, sugar, egg whites or egg substitute, and vanilla. Beat until smooth. Stir in oats and plumped raisins. Drop by rounded teaspoons onto a non-stick cookie sheet. Bake at 350 for about 10-12 minutes. Makes about 30 cookies.

Nutritional Analysis:	Original	Lowfat Version
Kcals. =	147	99
Chol. =	14 mg	0 mg
Sodium =	66 mg	32 mg
Fat =	6 grams	2 grams
Fat % =	37 %	20 %

PEANUT BUTTER OATMEAL COOKIES

Original Recipe:

¾ cup vegetable shortening
1 cup peanut butter
1 ½ cups brown sugar
½ cup water
1 egg
1 tsp. vanilla
3 cups old-fashioned oats
1 ½ cups flour
½ tsp. baking soda
1 cup raisins

Alterations:

* ¼ cup diet margarine
* ½ cup peanut butter
* ¾ cup brown sugar
*1 cup buttermilk (made from powdered)
*2 egg whites
*1 ½ tsps. vanilla

*1 ½ cups whole wheat pastry flour
*1 tsp. baking soda
*Soften raisins

Directions:

SOFTEN raisins in hot water; drain off water and use to make the cup of buttermilk. Cream the margarine, peanut butter, and brown sugar. Add the buttermilk, egg whites, and vanilla; beat until smooth. Combine oats, flour, and soda; add wet ingredients to dry ingredients and stir until mixed thoroughly. Add softened raisins, combining completely. Drop dough onto a non-stick cookie sheet and bake at 350 for about 10 to 12 minutes. Makes about 48 cookies.

Nutritional Analysis:

	Original	Lowfat Version
Kcals. =	121	78
Chol. =	4 mg	0 mg
Sodium =	40 mg	51 mg
Fat =	6 grams	2 grams
Fat % =	46 %	25 %

FARM STYLE
OATMEAL COOKIES

Original Recipe:

2 cups brown sugar
1 cup vegetable shortening
½ cup buttermilk
1 tsp. vanilla
4 cups oats
1 ¾ cup white flour
1 tsp. baking soda
¾ tsp. salt

Alterations:

*1 cup brown sugar
* ½ cup diet margarine
*1 cup buttermilk

*1 cup white + ¾ cup whole wheat

* ¼ tsp. salt or omit

Directions:

CREAM brown sugar and margarine. Add buttermilk and vanilla. Mix dry ingredients and blend with wet ingredients. Drop about a tablespoon of dough onto a non-stick cookie sheet and flatten slightly with the back of the spoon. Bake at 375 for about 10 minutes. Makes 40 - 50 cookies.

Nutritional Analysis:	Original	Lowfat Version
Kcals. =	111	65
Chol. =	0 mg	0 mg
Sodium =	55 mg	56 mg
Fat =	5 grams	1.4 grams
Fat % =	37 %	19 %

SNOWBALL COOKIES

Original Recipe:

1 cup vegetable shortening
3/4 cup powdered sugar
2 Tbls. water
1 1/2 tsp. vanilla
1 3/4 cup white flour

1/4 tsp. salt
1 cup rolled oats
1/2 cup chopped pecans
About 1/2 cup powdered sugar for coating cookies

Alterations:

*1 cup diet margarine

*1 tsp. vanilla + 1 tsp. walnut flavoring
*1 cup white
    + 3/4 cup pastry whole wheat
*Omit salt

*Omit

Directions:

HEAT oven to 325. Beat first four ingredients until creamy. Add flour and oats. Mix well. Shape into small balls (1 rounded teaspoon for each); bake on a non-stick cookie sheet for 15 to 18 minutes or until bottoms are light golden brown. Roll in powdered sugar while warm. Cool completely on a wire rack. Reroll in powdered sugar if desired. Makes about 48 small cookies.

Nutritional Analysis:

	Original	Lowfat Version
Kcals. =	83	53
Chol. =	0 mg	0 mg
Sodium =	11 mg	46 mg
Fat =	5 grams	2 grams
Fat % =	56 %	34 %

SUGAR PUFF COOKIES

Original Recipe:

3 cups sugar
1 ½ cups brown sugar
3 ⅓ cups vegetable shortening

3 eggs
6 cups flour
3 tsps. salt
6 tsps. baking soda
6 tsps. cream of tartar
6 tsps. vanilla

Alterations:

*1 ½ cups sugar
* ¾ cup brown sugar
*2 cups diet margarine + 1 cup nonfat
    cream cheese
*6 egg whites or ¾ cup Egg Beaters
*Optional - use half whole wheat
*1 tsp. salt or less

Directions:

CREAM margarine, nonfat cream cheese, and sugars; add egg whites or *Egg Beaters* and vanilla, and beat until fluffy. Combine dry ingredients and add to creamed mixture. Stir thoroughly. Bake cookies at 350 for 10-12 minutes on a non-stick cookie sheet. Makes 6 dozen cookies.

Nutritional Analysis:

	Original	Lowfat Version
Kcals. =	174	88
Chol. =	9 mg	0 mg
Sodium =	162 mg	167 mg
Fat =	10 grams	3 grams
Fat % =	50 %	26 %

DROP SUGAR
COOKIES

Original Ingredients:

1 cup butter
1 cup vegetable shortening
1 cup white sugar
1 cup brown sugar
2 eggs
4 ½ cups white flour
1 tsp. cream of tartar
¼ tsp. lemon extract
1 tsp. baking soda

Alterations:

*1 cup diet margarine
*Omit
* ½ cup white sugar
* ½ cup brown sugar
*4 egg whites
*Use 1 - 2 cups whole wheat flour

* ½ tsp. lemon extract

*1 tsp. butter flavoring

Directions:

CREAM margarine and sugars; add egg whites and flavorings and beat until combined. Mix flour, baking soda, and cream of tartar; add to creamed mixture and stir until a soft dough is formed. Roll dough into small balls and place on cookie sheets. Flatten balls with a glass dipped in sugar. Bake in a 350 oven for 10 minutes. Makes 48 large cookies.

Nutritional Analysis:

	Original	Lowfat Version
Kcals. =	151	77
Chol. =	10 mg	0 mg
Sodium =	54 mg	68 mg
Fat =	8 grams	2 grams
Fat % =	50 %	23 %

RICH CHOCOLATE
CHIP COOKIES

Original Recipe:

1 cup butter

1 cup white sugar
1 cup brown sugar
2 eggs
2 cups flour
1 tsp. baking powder
1 tsp. baking soda
2 ½ cups oats ground into flour in food processor
1 tsp. vanilla
12 oz. chocolate chips
18 oz. finely grated chocolate bar
1 ½ cups chopped nuts

Alterations:

* ½ cup diet margarine + ½ cup
nonfat yogurt or cream cheese

* ½ cup white sugar
* ½ cup brown sugar
*4 egg whites

*2 tsps. vanilla
*Or use 8 oz.
*Omit
* ⅓ cup chopped nuts or omit

Directions:

CREAM margarine, sugars, egg whites, and nonfat yogurt (use an electric mixer); add vanilla and set aside. Combine the flour, ground oats, baking powder, and baking soda; add to the creamed mixture along with the nuts and chocolate chips. Drop dough onto a non-stick or sprayed pan; dough will require flattening with the back of the spoon. Bake at 350 for about 10 minutes. Do not overbake. Let stand a couple of minutes before removing. Makes about 48 cookies.

Nutritional Analysis:

	Original	Altered Version
Kcals. =	193	104
Chol. =	19 mg	0 mg
Sodium =	89 mg	56 mg
Fat =	11 grams	4 grams
Fat % =	49 %	35 %

NOTE: Without nuts = 99 kcals., 3.75 grams fat, 33% fat

With 8 oz. chips = 92 kcals., 3.4 grams fat, 32 % fat

CINNAMON CHOCOLATE CHIP COOKIES

Original Recipe:

1 cup butter
½ cup shortening
1 ⅓ cups sugar
1 cup brown sugar
4 eggs

1 tsp. vanilla
1 tsp. lemon juice
3 cups flour
2 tsps. baking powder
1 ½ tsps. salt
1 tsp. cinnamon
½ cup rolled oats
12 oz. chocolate chips
1 cup chopped nuts

Alterations:

* ½ cup diet margarine
*1 cup nonfat cream cheese
* ⅔ cup sugar
* ½ cup brown sugar
*1 cup Egg Beaters or 4 egg whites +
    ½ cup nonfat milk
*1 tsp. butter flavoring + 1 tsp. vanilla

*Use half whole wheat

*Reduce to ¼ tsp. or omit
*2 tsps. cinnamon

*6 oz. chocolate chips
*Reduce to ½ cup or omit

Directions:

CREAM margarine, nonfat cream cheese, and sugars; beat well. Add egg whites, milk, vanilla, butter flavoring, and lemon juice. Add flours, soda, salt, and cinnamon. Mix in oats, nuts, and chips. Drop onto a non-stick cookie sheet. Bake at 350 for about 15 minutes. Makes 5 dozen (60 cookies).

Nutritional Analysis:

	Original	Lowfat Version	
		(Nuts)	(Without Nuts)
Kcals. =	145	71	65
Chol. =	14 mg	0 mg	0 mg
Sodium =	107 mg	40 mg	40 mg
Fat =	8.5 grams	2.5 grams	2 grams
Fat % =	51 %	30 %	25 %

MOCHA CHOCOLATE CHIP COOKIES

Original Recipe:

½ cup margarine
½ cup semisweet chocolate chips

1 Tbls. instant coffee crystals
¾ cup sugar
¾ cup brown sugar
2 eggs
2 tsps. vanilla
2 cups flour
⅓ cup cocoa powder
½ tsp. baking powder
¼ tsp. salt
1 cup semisweet chocolate chips

Alterations:

* ½ cup diet margarine
* ¼ cup chocolate chips + ¼ cup skim milk

*Omit

*4 egg whites or ½ cup Egg Beaters

*Use ½ to 1 cup whole wheat

*Omit
* ½ cup chocolate chips

Directions:

IN a non-stick saucepan melt margarine and the ¼ cup chocolate chips + ¼ cup skim milk over low heat. Remove from heat and stir in coffee crystals; cool 5 minutes. Stir in sugar, egg substitute or egg whites, and vanilla. Combine flour, cocoa powder, and baking powder. Stir into coffee mixture. Stir in the remaining ½ cup of chocolate chips. Drop dough by rounded tablespoons onto a non-stick cookie sheet. Bake in 350 oven 10 minutes. Let cool one minute before removing from sheet. Makes 30 cookies.

Nutritional Analysis:

	Original	Lowfat Version
Kcals. =	143	90
Chol. =	0 mg	0 mg
Sodium =	70 mg	53 mg
Fat =	6 grams	3 grams
Fat % =	37 %	31 %

ORANGE CHOCOLATE CHIP COOKIES

Ingredients:

⅔ cup brown sugar
⅔ cup diet margarine
2 Tbls. grated orange peel
4 egg whites or ½ cup Egg Beaters
1 tsp. vanilla
1 tsp. orange extract
1 tsp. baking soda
1 cup + 2 Tbls. white flour
1 cup + 2 Tbls. wheat pastry flour
3 cups corn flakes (or other flake type cereal), crushed
½ cup mini-chocolate chips

Directions:

CREAM margarine and sugar; add orange peel, egg whites, and flavorings. Combine dry ingredients plus crushed corn flakes and chocolate chips. Add wet ingredients to dry and stir to combine (dough will be fairly stiff). Bake at 375 for about 10 minutes. Makes 40 - 48 cookies.

Nutritional Analysis: (based on 48 cookies)

Kcals. =	58
Chol. =	0 mg
Sodium =	68 mg
Fat =	2 grams
Fat % =	29 %

NOTE: It is much easier and quicker to grate orange peel using the large shredder (as for shredded cheese). Freeze any extra peel in an air tight container.

MOCK MACAROONS

Original Recipe:

1 cup vegetable shortening

1 cup brown sugar
1 cup white sugar
2 eggs, slightly beaten
1 tsp. vanilla

2 cups corn flakes
2 cups shredded coconut
2 cups flour
1 tsp. baking soda
1 tsp. baking powder
½ tsp. salt

Alterations:

* ½ cup diet margarine + ½ cup nonfat cream cheese

* ½ cup brown sugar
* ½ cup white sugar
*4 egg whites
*Plus 1 tsp. each almond and coconut flavoring
*3 cups corn flakes
*1 cup shredded coconut
*Half whole wheat/half white

*Omit

Directions:

CREAM the margarine, nonfat cream cheese, and sugars; add the egg whites, vanilla, almond, and coconut flavoring, beating until smooth. Combine the flours, baking powder, and baking soda and add to wet ingredients. Stir until thoroughly combined; add the coconut and cornflakes; mix and drop by rounded teaspoons onto a non-stick baking sheet. Bake at 375 for 12 minutes or until golden brown. Makes 48 small cookies. NOTE: These cookies will spread as they bake, no need to flatten.

Nutritional Analysis:

	Original	Lowfat Version
Kcals. =	116	61
Chol. =	9 mg	7 mg
Sodium =	71 mg	74 mg
Fat =	6 grams	2 grams
Fat % =	45 %	25 %

CHOCOLATE - JAM
COOKIES

Original Recipe:

1 cup margarine	
¾ cup brown sugar	
2 egg yolks	
2 oz. semisweet chocolate, melted	
1 ½ tsp. finely shredded orange peel	
1 tsp. cinnamon	
1 tsp. vanilla	
¼ tsp. salt	
2 ¼ cups flour	
1 ½ - 2 cups chopped pecans	
2 egg whites	
¾ cup cherry jam	

Alterations:

* *½ cup diet margarine + ½ cup nonfat cream cheese*
* *½ cup brown sugar*
* *¼ cup* Egg Beaters
*Or use chocolate chips

*Omit
*Use 1 cup whole wheat
* *½ cup chopped walnuts or omit*
*Omit
*Use reduced sugar jam

Directions:

COMBINE margarine and brown sugar; beat well. Add *Egg Beaters* and beat again. Blend in melted chocolate, orange peel, cinnamon, and vanilla. Stir in flours and nuts. Shape dough into 1-inch balls and place on a non-stick baking sheet. Using your thumb, make a slight depression in top of each cookie. Bake in 350 oven about 10 minutes. Cool and fill centers with a small spoonful of jam. Makes 60 cookies.

Nutritional Analysis:	Original	Lowfat Version
Kcals. =	93	55
Chol. =	7 mg	0 mg
Sodium =	49 mg	25 mg
Fat =	6 grams	2 grams
Fat % =	53 %	28 %

EASY BROWNIES

Original Recipe:

4 eggs

2 cups sugar
1 ⅓ cups oil
½ cup cocoa powder
2 tsps. vanilla
2 cups flour
1 ½ tsps. salt
1 tsp. baking powder

Alterations:

*1 cup Egg Beaters *or* ½ cup
   Egg Beaters + ½ cup vanilla or
   plain nonfat yogurt

*1 cup sugar
* ⅓ cup canola oil + 1 cup applesauce

*Use half white/half whole wheat
*Omit salt

Directions:

COMBINE all ingredients and bake in a non-stick 9X13 inch pan for 25-30 minutes at 325. Makes 16 brownies.

Nutritional Analysis:

	Original	Lowfat Version
Kcals. =	339	167
Chol. =	53 mg	0 mg
Sodium =	237 mg	50 mg
Fat =	20 grams	5 grams
Fat % =	52 %	27 %

QUICK FUDGE BROWNIES

Original Recipe:

2 egg whites
½ cup unsweetened applesauce
½ cup water
Packaged light brownie mix

Directions:

PREHEAT oven to 350. Spray a 9X13 inch baking pan. Mix brownie mix, water, applesauce, and egg whites in a large bowl. Beat 50 strokes by hand (do not undermix).

SPREAD in pan and bake for 25 minutes. Do not overbake. Cool completely and store in an airtight container or freeze. Makes 24 brownies.

OPTIONAL: Frost lightly with a mixture of 1 cup powdered sugar, 1 tablespoon cocoa, 1 tsp. vanilla, and enough skim milk to make spreadable but fairly thick. Frost brownies while warm. Cool uncovered. Store in the freezer. 24 servings.

Nutritional Analysis:

Kcals. =	104
Chol. =	0 mg
Sodium =	97 mg
Fat =	1 gram
Fat % =	12 %

FROSTED FUDGE BROWNIES

Original Recipe:

½ cup margarine or butter
2 oz. unsweetened chocolate
1 cup sugar
2 eggs
1 tsp. vanilla
¾ cup flour
½ cup chopped nuts
½ recipe chocolate frosting

Alterations:

* ½ cup diet margarine
*2 - 4 Tbls. cocoa powder

*4 egg whites or ½ cup Egg Beaters
*1 - 2 tsps. vanilla

* ¼ cup chopped nuts
*Use lowfat version (see next page)

Directions:

CREAM margarine, cocoa, and sugar. Add egg substitute or egg whites and vanilla; beat lightly by hand until combined. Stir in flour and nuts. Spread batter into a nonstick 8X8 inch pan. Bake at 350 for 30 minutes. Frost top, cool, and cut into 12 bars.

Nutritional Analysis:

	Original	Lowfat Version
Kcals. =	290	177
Chol. =	60 mg	0 mg
Sodium =	89 mg	114 mg
Fat =	17 grams	5 grams
Fat % –	51 %	27 %

NONFAT CHOCOLATE FROSTING

Original Recipe:

4 oz. semisweet chocolate, cut up
3 Tbls. margarine or butter
1 ½ cups powdered sugar

Alterations:

*2 Tbls. cocoa powder
*2 Tbls. nonfat cream cheese

*1 ½ tsps. vanilla + ½ tsp. butter
flavoring

Directions:

COMBINE the above ingredients. Frosting will be thick; spread over top of cake while warm. Let cake cool and frosting dry completely. Can be stored for one day by covering completely cooled cake with a layer of waxed paper and then foil. Store frosted cake in the freezer for longer than one day.

Enough frosting to cover tops of two 8 or 9-inch cake layers or one 10-inch tube cake.

Nutritional Analysis:

(12 Servings)	Original	Lowfat Version
Kcals. =	121	52
Chol. =	8 mg	0 mg
Sodium =	26 mg	2 mg
Fat =	6 grams	0 grams
Fat % =	44 %	3 %

LEMON BARS

Original Recipe:

2 cups flour
½ cup powdered sugar
1 cup butter
⅛ tsp. salt
4 beaten eggs
½ cup lemon juice
2 cups sugar
¼ cup flour
½ tsp. baking powder

Alterations:

*Use half whole wheat or oat

* ½ cup diet margarine
*Omit salt
*1 cup Egg Beaters

*1 cup sugar
* ¼ cup cornstarch

Directions:

COMBINE flour and powdered sugar; cut margarine in with a fork. Press mixture into a 9X13 non-stick baking pan. Beat *Egg Beaters*, lemon juice, sugar, cornstarch, and baking powder until smooth. Pour on top of crust and bake at 350 for 25 minutes. Top with powdered sugar when cool. Serves 12.

Nutritional Analysis:	Original	Lowfat Version
Kcals. =	393	212
Chol. =	112 mg	0 mg
Sodium =	188 mg	142 mg
Fat =	17 grams	3 grams
Fat % =	39 %	17 %

LIGHT CRANBERRY BARS

Original Recipe:

1 ½ cups flour + 2 Tbls. divided (use half white/half whole wheat pastry flour)
1 Tbls. sugar
1 16 oz. can whole-berry cranberry sauce
1 Tbls. fresh lemon juice
1 tsp. grated orange peel
2 ½ cups old fashioned oats
½ cup packed brown sugar
½ tsp. baking soda
1 tsp. ground cinnamon
⅛ tsp. salt
½ cup diet margarine
½ cup buttermilk (made from powdered)
1 egg white, lightly beaten

Directions:

MIX 1 tablespoon each sugar, white flour, and whole wheat pastry flour and set aside.

In a non-stick saucepan over medium heat, bring cranberry sauce to a boil; add the flour and sugar mixture. Simmer over low heat, stirring until thickened; add lemon juice and orange peel. Cool slightly.

COMBINE oats, remaining flours, brown sugar, baking soda, cinnamon, and salt. Using a wooden spoon, stir in margarine, buttermilk, and egg white until mixture is crumbly. Press half of dough evenly into a non-stick 9X13 pan; spread cranberry filling over dough and top with remaining dough. Bake at 350 for 30 to 35 minutes. Cool and cut into 24 bars.

Nutritional Analysis:

Kcals. =	129
Chol. =	0 mg
Sodium =	90 mg
Fat =	3 grams
Fat % =	17 %

DRIED FRUIT NEWTONS

Original Recipe:

1 cup whole wheat flour
1 1/4 cups white flour
1/4 cup wheat germ
1/4 tsp. salt
1/4 tsp. baking soda
1/2 cup margarine
1/2 cup white sugar
1/2 cup brown sugar
2 eggs
1/2 tsp. vanilla

Alterations:

*2 cups whole wheat flour
*1 cup white flour

*Omit
* 1/2 tsp. baking soda
* 1/2 cup diet margarine

*4 egg whites

Filling :

1 lb. figs, chopped
1/2 cup chopped walnuts
1/3 cup white sugar
1/2 cup water
1 tsp. lemon peel
2 Tbls. lemon juice

*1 1/4 lb. figs, chopped
*Omit

Directions:

COMBINE DRY INGREDIENTS: Beat margarine, sugars, vanilla, and egg whites. Stir in flour mixture and knead dough until smooth. Cover and chill at least one hour.

PREPARE FILLING: Chop figs in food processor and mix with water, 1/3 cup sugar, lemon peel, and lemon juice. Cook until mixture thickens, about 8 minutes. Cool.

ROLL out dough (on a floured board) half at a time into two 9X15 rectangles; cut into strips (6 total). Distribute filling down each strip evenly. Using a long spatula, lift sides of each dough strip over filling, overlapping slightly on top. Press together lightly. Cut strips in half; lift and invert, seam side down, onto a non-stick baking sheet. Brush off excess flour. Chill for about 15 minutes. Bake at 375 for about 15 to 20 minutes. Cool and cut each strip into 4 pieces. Makes 4 dozen (store in freezer). NOTE: Other dried fruits can be used; such as prunes, apricots or dates.

Nutritional Analysis:

	Original	Lowfat Version
Kcals. =	79 grams	62
Chol. =	9 mg	0 mg
Sodium =	42 mg	38 mg
Fat =	3 grams	1 gram
Fat % =	33 %	15 %

COCKEYED CAKE

Original Recipe:

1 ½ cups flour
3 Tbls. cocoa powder
1 tsp. soda
1 cup sugar
½ tsp. salt
5 Tbls. canola oil
1 Tbls. vinegar
1 tsp. vanilla
1 cup cold water

Alterations:

*Use ½ cup whole wheat or oat flour

*Reduce sugar to ½ cup
*Reduce salt to ⅛ tsp.
*2 Tbls. canola oil + 3 Tbls. applejuice

Directions:

COMBINE flour, cocoa powder, soda, sugar, and salt. Make a well in dry ingredients and add all wet ingredients. Stir to combine. Pour into a non-stick 8X8 inch pan and bake at 350 for about 30 minutes. Serves 6.

Nutritional Analysis:

	Original	Lowfat Version
Kcals. =	350	229
Chol. =	0 mg	0 mg
Sodium =	318 mg	186 mg
Fat =	12 grams	5 grams
Fat % =	31 %	21 %

SOUR CREAM FUDGE CAKE

Original Recipe:

2 oz. unsweetened chocolate
2 cups white flour
1 ½ cups sugar
1 tsp. baking soda
½ cup shortening
1 ¼ cups sour cream
2 eggs
1 tsp. vanilla
¼ cup hot water

Alterations:

*4 Tbls. cocoa powder
*Use half whole wheat
* ¾ cup sugar

* ½ cup diet margarine
*Use nonfat yogurt
* ½ Egg Beaters

Filling or Topping:

4 oz. chocolate chips
¼ cup butter
⅓ cup powdered sugar
1 egg yolk
1 tsp. vanilla
1 egg white
2 cups whipped cream

* ¼ cup nonfat cream cheese

* ⅛ cup Egg Beaters

*Omit

Directions:

PREHEAT oven to 350. Spray two 8X1½ inch layer cake pans with vegetable spray. Combine flour, sugar, soda, and cocoa. Cream margarine with yogurt; add ½ cup egg substitute, vanilla, and hot water. Add dry ingredients to wet ingredients and beat until smooth. Pour batter into pans evenly and bake for 30 - 35 minutes. Cool for 10 – 20 minutes; Split the layers with a long serrated knife and spread fudge filling (see below) between layers. Serves 12.

FILLING: Melt chocolate chips; beat nonfat cream cheese with sugar until fluffy. Add ⅛ cup egg substitute and beat well. Stir in chocolate and vanilla. Beat egg white until stiff and fold into mix. Store in refrigerator until cake is cool. Spread between layers.

NOTE: This cake can also be prepared in a 9X13 pan. Serve with the fudge filling spooned over the top of each piece.

Nutritional Analysis:

	Original	Lowfat Version
Kcals. =	503	244
Chol. =	101 mg	1 mg
Sodium =	317 mg	211 mg
Fat =	31 grams	8 grams
Fat % =	56 %	27 %

MISSISSIPPI FUDGE CAKE

Original Recipe:

1 cup margarine

4 eggs
2 cups white sugar
1 ½ cups white flour
⅓ cup cocoa powder
1 Tbls. vanilla
1 cup chopped walnuts
½ cup shredded coconut
7 oz. marshmallow creme

Alterations:

* ½ cup diet margarine +½ cup apple-
    sauce or mashed banana
*1 cup Egg Beaters
*1 cup white sugar
*1 cup white / ½ cup whole wheat

*Omit or ½ cup chopped walnuts

Frosting:

½ cup margarine
½ cup canned milk

16 oz. powdered sugar
1 tsp. vanilla

*3 Tbls. evaporated skim or nonfat cream
    cheese
*2 cups powdered sugar
*1 tsp. vanilla

Directions:

COMBINE all ingredients except marshmallow creme, place in a sprayed or non-stick 9X13 pan and bake at 350 for 35 minutes. Smooth marshmallow creme OR nonfat frosting over cake immediately upon removing from the oven. Put in refrigerator to cool and set. Serves 12.

Nutritional Analysis:

	Original		Lowfat Version	
	w/cream	w/frosting	w/cream	w/frosting
Kcals. =	488	663	279	294
Chol. =	71 mg	74 mg	0 mg	0 mg
Sodium =	221 mg	313 mg	149 mg	145 mg
Fat =	25 grams	33 grams	9 grams	9 grams
Fat % =	45 %	44 %	27 %	26 %

BECKY'S BEST CHOCOLATE CAKE

Original Recipe:

3/4 cup shortening
1 1/2 cups sugar
3 eggs, well beaten
1 3/4 cups flour
1/2 tsp. baking powder
1/2 tsp. baking soda
1/2 tsp. salt
3/4 tsp. nutmeg
1 tsp. cinnamon
2 Tbls. cocoa powder
3/4 cup buttermilk
1 tsp. each vanilla & lemon extract
3/4 cup chopped walnuts

Alterations:

* 1/2 cup diet margarine
* 3/4 cup sugar
* 3/4 cup Egg Beaters
*Use 3/4 cup pastry whole wheat
*1 tsp. baking powder

*Omit

*1 cup buttermilk

* 1/3 cup chopped walnuts

Frosting:

6 Tbls. butter

3 cups powdered sugar
1 egg yolk
1 1/2 Tbls. cocoa powder
1 tsp. cinnamon
1 Tbls. strong coffee

*2 Tbls. evaporated skim milk or nonfat
*   cream cheese*
*2 cups powdered sugar
*Omit
*4 Tbls. cocoa powder
*+ 1/2 tsp. each butter & vanilla flavoring
*2 tsp. strong coffee

Directions:

CREAM diet margarine and sugar until light and fluffy. Blend in egg substitute. Combine flour, baking powder, baking soda, spices, nuts, and cocoa powder. Add to creamed mixture alternately with buttermilk. Pour batter into a non-stick 9X13 pan. Bake at 350 for about 30 minutes. Prepare frosting and smooth on cake while still warm. Let cake cool and cut into squares. Serves 12. FOR FROSTING: Combine all dry ingredients with the wet ingredients until smooth. Do not overmix; spread on warm cake immediately.

Nutritional Analysis:

	Original	Lowfat Version
Kcals. =	507	261
Chol. =	87 mg	1 mg
Sodium =	220 mg	206 mg
Fat =	26 grams	7 grams
Fat %	44 %	

Fat % =   44 %   22 %

CHOCOLATE ZUCCHINI CAKE

Original Recipe:

½ cup soft margarine
½ cup vegetable oil
1 ¾ cups sugar
2 whole eggs
1 tsp. vanilla
½ cup milk + 1 tsp. lemon juice
2 ½ cups flour

4 Tbls. cocoa powder
½ tsp. baking powder
1 tsp. baking soda
1 tsp. salt
½ tsp. cinnamon
½ tsp. cloves
2 cups finely shredded zucchini
¾ cup chocolate chips

Alterations:

* *½ cup diet margarine*
* *½ cup unsweetened applesauce*
**1 cup sugar*
**4 egg whites*

**Use nonfat milk*
**Use 1 ½ cups white + 1 cup whole wheat*

**Omit*
**1 tsp. cinnamon*
**1 tsp. cloves*

* *½ cup chocolate chips*

Directions:

CREAM margarine, applesauce, and sugar; add egg whites, vanilla, and sour milk. Mix all dry ingredients together. Add to creamed mixture; beat well with mixer. Stir in shredded zucchini. Spoon batter into sprayed 9X13 pan and sprinkle top with chocolate chips. Bake at 325 for 40- 45 minutes. Serves 12.

Nutritional Analysis:	Original	Altered Version
Kcals. =	436	246
Chol. =	37 mg	0 mg
Sodium =	381 mg	200 mg
Fat =	22 grams	7 grams
Fat % =	45 %	24 %

BEACH BIRTHDAY
CAKE

Original Recipe:

Alterations:

Topping:

2/3 cup chocolate chips
1/2 cup graham cracker crumbs
1/3 cup melted butter
1/2 cup chopped walnuts

* 1/3 cup mini-chocolate chips

*2 Tbls. melted diet margarine
* 1/4 cup chopped walnuts

Cake:

1/3 cup chocolate chips, melted
2 cups flour
1 tsp. soda
1 tsp. salt
1 1/2 cups + 2 Tbls. sugar
1/2 cup butter

2 eggs
1 tsp. vanilla
1 cup milk + 1 Tbls. vinegar
1 cup whipping cream

*Half white/half whole wheat

* 1/4 tsp. salt or omit
* 3/4 cup sugar
* 1/4 cup diet margarine + 1/4 cup
*   nonfat yogurt*
*4 egg whites or 1/2 cup Egg Beaters

*Use nonfat milk
*One package Dream Whip + 1/2 cup
*   skim milk + 1/2 tsp. vanilla*

Directions:

COMBINE graham cracker crumbs, melted margarine, walnuts, and mini-chips. Set aside. Combine flour with soda. Cream margarine and sugar; add egg whites, melted chips, and vanilla. Add dry ingredients alternately with milk/vinegar mixture. Pour batter into two 9-inch round layer pans (non-stick or sprayed). Sprinkle tops of both pans with crumb mixture. Bake at 375 for 30 to 40 minutes. Frost with *Dream Whip* between layers and on the sides. Serves 12.

Nutritional Analysis:	Original	Lowfat Version
Kcals. =	511	270
Chol. =	100 mg	1 mg
Sodium =	415 mg	255 mg
Fat =	31 grams	10 grams
Fat % =	52 %	31 %

CHOCOLATE DECADENCE CAKE

Original Recipe:

1 cup boiling water
3 ounces unsweetened chocolate
½ cup butter
1 tsp. vanilla
2 cups sugar
2 eggs, separated
1 tsp. baking soda
½ cup sour cream
2 cups less 2 Tbls. flour
1 tsp. baking powder

Alterations:

*4 Tbls. cocoa powder
* ½ cup diet margarine

*1 cup sugar
* ¼ cup Egg Beaters + 2 egg whites

* ½ cup nonfat yogurt

Frosting: (enough for two cakes)

2 Tbls. sweet butter
¾ cup semisweet chocolate chips
6 Tbls. heavy cream
1 ¼ cups powdered sugar
1 tsp. vanilla

*Omit

*6 Tbls. nonfat cream cheese

*1 tsp. each butter flavoring and vanilla

Directions:

PREHEAT oven to 350. Spray and flour a 10-inch tube pan. Pour boiling water over diet margarine and let stand until melted. Stir in vanilla and sugar; whisk in *Egg Beaters*, blending well. Combine baking soda and nonfat yogurt and whisk into sugar/egg mixture. Sift flour, cocoa, and baking powder together and add to wet ingredients mixing thoroughly. Beat egg whites until stiff but not dry. Stir a quarter of the egg whites thoroughly into the batter. Spoon remaining egg whites on top of the batter and gently fold together. Pour batter into the prepared pan. Set on the middle rack of the oven and bake for 40 to 50 minutes, or until the edges have pulled away from the sides of the pan. Cool in pan for 10 minutes; unmold and cool before frosting. 12 servings.

FROSTING DIRECTIONS: Place the chocolate chips, flavorings, and nonfat cream cheese in a microwave dish. Microwave on high for 2 minutes. Stir until smooth and add the powdered sugar. Again, stir until smooth. Cool briefly and frost cake while frosting is still warm. MAKES ENOUGH FROSTING FOR 2 CAKES. Freeze leftover frosting.

Continued on next page

Chocolate Decadence Cake – continued

Nutritional Analysis:	Original	Lowfat Version
Kcals. =	478	239
Chol. =	79 mg	0 mg
Sodium =	198 mg	219 mg
Fat =	23 grams	6 grams
Fat % =	41 %	22 %

ADAPTED FROM THE SILVER PALATE COOKBOOK

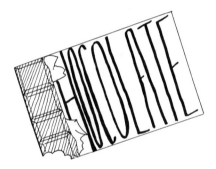

LEMONADE ANGEL DESSERT

Ingredients:

1 envelope unflavored gelatin
½ cup sugar
Dash of salt
2 beaten eggs
½ cup water
6 oz. can frozen lemonade concentrate
14 ½ oz. evaporated skim milk; chilled in freezer and whipped
Yellow food coloring
10-inch angel cake

Directions:

THOROUGHLY mix gelatin, sugar, and salt; add eggs and water. Cook over medium heat and stir until gelatin dissolves and mixture thickens slightly; remove from heat. Stir in lemonade concentrate. Chill until partially set; fold into whipped evaporated skim milk (must be chilled & icy cold in order to whip). Add a few drops of yellow food coloring. Tear the cake into bite-size pieces. Cover bottom of a 10-inch tube pan with a thin layer of the gelatin mixture. Then arrange ⅓ of the cake on top. Pour ⅓ of remaining gelatin over. Repeat layers. Chill until firm. Unmold on serving plate. Serves 12.

Nutritional Analysis:

Kcals. =	224
Chol. =	37 mg
Sodium =	343 mg
Fat =	1 gram
Fat % =	4 %

EASY RUM CAKE

Ingredients:

½ cup chopped walnuts
1 yellow Lovin Lites *cake mix*
1 package vanilla instant pudding mix
4 egg whites + ½ cup Egg Beaters
1 cup water
½ cup apple juice
2 tsps. rum flavoring

Directions:

SPRINKLE nuts over bottom of a sprayed bundt cake pan. Combine cake mix, pudding mix, egg whites, egg substitute, water, juice, and rum flavoring. Mix thoroughly with a beater. Pour batter over nuts. Bake for about 1 hour at 325. Invert cake onto serving plate after cooling slightly.

GLAZE:

¼ cup diet margarine
1 cup apple juice
1 tsp. rum flavoring
1 tsp. butter flavoring

BOIL the above ingredients for 5 minutes. With an ice pick, prick holes in the top and sides of the cake. Drizzle all of the glaze over the top and sides of cake, allowing it to be absorbed. Serves 12. Delicious served warm or cool.

Nutritional Analysis:

Kcals. =	236
Chol. =	0 mg
Sodium =	317 mg
Fat =	5 grams
Fat % =	21 %

LEMON SPONGE CAKE

Original Recipe:

1 cup sugar
3 Tbls. flour
3 Tbls. butter
2 eggs
1 cup milk
Grated rind and juice of one lemon
Single pie crust, baked

Alterations:

* 1/2 cup sugar

*3 Tbls. diet margarine
* 1/4 cup Egg Beaters + 2 egg whites
*Use nonfat milk
*About 1 - 2 Tbls. rind + 1/4 cup juice
*15 graham crackers, crushed or whole

Directions:

WITH an electric mixer combine the sugar, flour, margarine, egg substitute, lemon juice, and rind. Beat egg whites until stiff and fold into mixture. Pour over graham crackers that have been placed on the bottom of a non-stick 8-inch pan (or pour over a prepared graham cracker crust using the 15 crushed crackers mixed with 1 1/2 Tbls. melted diet margarine). Bake at 350 for 30 to 45 minutes. Serves 6.

Nutritional Analysis:

	Original	Lowfat Version
Kcals. =	397	211
Chol. =	92 mg	0 mg
Sodium =	273 mg	189 mg
Fat =	19 grams	3 grams
Fat % =	42 %	12 %

BANANA NUT CAKE

Original Ingredients:

½ cup butter
1 ½ cups sugar
2 eggs
2 cups flour
1 tsp. soda
1 tsp. baking powder
1 cup nuts
1 cup chocolate chips
3 large ripe bananas
½ cup milk
1 tsp. vanilla

Alterations:

*½ cup diet margarine
*¾ cup (scant) sugar
*4 egg whites or ½ cup Egg Beaters
*1 cup white/1 cup whole wheat flour

*Omit or use less (see below)
*1 cup chocolate chips or less

*½ cup nonfat milk
*1 tsp. vanilla + 1 tsp. walnut flavoring

Directions:

CREAM diet margarine, sugar, and egg substitute or egg whites. Combine flour, soda, baking powder, and chocolate chips (also add nuts if desired). Mash bananas and combine with milk and flavorings (use walnut flavoring if omitting nuts). Combine creamed mixtures and flour alternately. Bake in a non-stick bundt pan at 350 for 50 minutes. Serve warm or cool. Makes 12 servings.

Nutritional Analysis:

	Original	Lowfat Version
Kcals. =	421	260
Chol. =	58 mg	0 mg
Sodium =	180 mg	213 mg
Fat =	20 grams	9 grams
Fat % =	42 %	30 %

Options:

#1 = Omit choc. chips
       Add ½ cup nuts   = 221 kcals.
                                 7 grams fat
                                 28 % fat

#2 = Use ¼ cup nuts &   = 240 kcals.
       ½ cup choc. chips   8 grams fat
                                 29 % fat

NOTE: If you decide to add some nuts, omit the walnut flavoring.

LITE SURPRISE BUNDT CAKE

Ingredients:

1 package Lovin Lites *chocolate cake mix*
½ cup chopped dried apricots (or raisins, currants, prunes)
½ cup chocolate chips or mini-chocolate chips
1 Tbls. cornstarch
4 egg whites or ½ cup Egg Beaters
1 ½ cups buttermilk
½ cup chopped walnuts (optional)
½ cup powdered sugar
1 tsp. vanilla + 1 tsp. water or milk

Directions:

COMBINE dried fruit, chocolate chips, walnuts, and cornstarch in a small bowl; stir to coat and set aside. Combine all remaining ingredients (except powdered sugar, vanilla, and water) in a large mixing bowl; mix on slow speed until blended. Fold in the fruit mixture until no longer white in color. Pour into a non-stick or sprayed bundt pan and bake for 40 - 50 minutes at 350.

COOL in the pan for about 15 minutes. Glaze with the powdered sugar, vanilla, and water mixture. Serves 12.

Nutritional Analysis:	With Nuts	Without Nuts
Kcals. =	353	322
Chol. =	1 mg	1 mg
Sodium =	230 mg	230 mg
Fat =	9 grams	6 grams
Fat % =	22 %	17 %

ADAPTED FROM SIMPLY COLORADO COOKBOOK

IRISH APPLE CAKE

Original Recipe:

4 cups diced apples
1 1/2 cups sugar
1/2 cup oil
1/2 cup chopped walnuts
2 tsp. vanilla
2 cups flour
1 tsp. cinnamon
2 tsp. baking soda
1/2 tsp. salt

Icing:

1/4 stick margarine
1/2 cup sugar

Alterations:

* 3/4 cup sugar
* 1/4 cup oil + 1/4 cup apple juice
*Reduce to 1/4 cup or omit

*Use 1/2 cup finely ground whole wheat

* 1/4 tsp. salt or less

*2 Tbls. diet margarine

Directions:

MIX apples and sugar; let stand while preparing remaining ingredients. Combine oil, apple juice, vanilla, and nuts (optional). Mix flour, cinnamon, soda, and salt. Stir dry ingredients into wet ingredients; add apples and combine. Pour into a non-stick or sprayed 9X13 pan and bake at 350 for about 50 minutes. Boil the sugar and diet margarine; pour over hot cake. Serves 12.

Nutritional Analysis:

	Original	Lowfat Version	
		(Nuts)	(Without Nuts)
Kcals. =	387	261	229
Chol. =	0 mg	0 mg	0 mg
Sodium =	250 mg	206 mg	205 mg
Fat =	18 grams	9 grams	6 grams
Fat % =	39 %	30 %	22 %

CARROT CAKE

Original Recipe:

2 cups sugar
1 1/3 cups oil
4 eggs, slightly beaten
2 cups white flour
1 tsp. salt
2 tsps. baking soda
2 tsps. cinnamon
3 cups raw carrots, finely shredded
1/2 cup chopped walnuts
8 oz. crushed pineapple, drained

Cream Cheese Frosting:

8 oz. cream cheese
1 lb. powdered sugar
2 tsps. vanilla
1/4 cup butter
2 Tbls. milk

Alterations:

* 1 cup sugar
* 1/3 cup canola oil
*1 cup Egg Beaters
*2 cups white + 1 cup whole wheat
* 1/4 tsp. salt
*3 tsps. baking soda

*Optional
*20 oz. crushed pineapple, undrained

* 1/4 cup nonfat cream cheese
*3 cups powdered sugar

*Omit
*Omit

Directions:

BEAT egg substitute, oil, and sugar. Combine flours, salt, soda, and cinnamon and add to egg mixture. Fold in carrots, nuts, and pineapple. Bake in a 9X13 non-stick pan at 300 for 60 minutes. Prepare frosting and top cake with it after it is cool. Serves 12, generously. Warm each piece in the microwave immediately before serving.

Nutritional Analysis:

	Original	Lowfat Version
Kcals. =	746	411
Chol. =	92 mg	0 mg
Sodium =	449 mg	303 mg
Fat =	40 grams	10 grams
Fat % =	47 %	20 %

COCONUT CARROT CAKE

Original Recipe:

3 eggs, beaten
2 cups sugar
2 cups flour
2 tsps. cinnamon
2 tsps. soda
1 tsp. salt
1 1/2 cup canola oil

2 cups grated carrots
1 cup raisins
1 cup less 2 Tbls. crushed pineapple
1 cup coconut

Alterations:

* 3/4 cup Egg Beaters or 6 whites
* 1/2 - 1 cup sugar
*Half whole wheat

*Reduce to 1/4 tsp. or less
* 1/2 cup canola oil + 1 cup pineapple juice

* 1/2 cup coconut

Nonfat Cream Cheese Frosting:

2 Tbls. crushed pineapple, drained
3 oz. cream cheese
1/4 cup soft butter

1/2 tsp. vanilla
1/2 lb. powdered sugar (2 cups)

*2–3 oz. nonfat cream cheese
*Omit butter; add 1/2 tsp. butter flavoring

*If frosting seems too thin, add a little more powdered sugar

Directions:

COMBINE egg whites or *Egg Beaters*, oil, pineapple juice, and sugar. Mix flour, cinnamon, soda, and salt; add to wet ingredients. Fold in carrots, coconut, raisins, and pineapple. Bake at 350 for one hour. Cool and frost with cream cheese frosting. Serves 12.

Nutritional Analysis:	Original	Lowfat Version
Kcals. =	697	397
Chol. =	71 mg	0 mg
Sodium =	413 mg	194 mg
Fat =	38 grams	11 grams
Fat % =	48 %	24 %

PEAR UPSIDE DOWN CAKE

Ingredients:

2 tsps. canola oil or walnut oil
⅓ cup brown sugar
2 D'Anjou or Bartlett Pears, cored and sliced
¾ cup + 2 Tbls. whole wheat pastry flour (or use half white)
¼ cup + 2 Tbls. cornmeal
2 - 3 Tbls. brown sugar
1 tsp. baking powder
1 tsp. baking soda
¾ tsp. cinnamon
1 Tbls. diet margarine
1 Tbls. canola oil or walnut oil
⅓ cup nonfat yogurt
⅓ cup water
½ tsp. butter flavoring

Directions:

PLACE 2 teaspoons canola oil in a non-stick 8X8 inch pan; make sure pan is coated and then sprinkle with the ⅓ cup brown sugar. Slice the pears (peel if using D'Anjou pears) and layer over top the brown sugar. Set aside.

COMBINE the flour, cornmeal, brown sugar, baking powder, baking soda, and cinnamon; cut in the margarine and canola oil until crumbly. Mix the yogurt and water; add to the dry mixture and stir to combine. Spread over the pears and bake at 425 for 20 to 25 minutes. Serve warm with nonfat milk or frozen vanilla nonfat yogurt. Makes 6 serving.

Nutritional Analysis:

Kcals. =	252
Chol. =	0 mg
Sodium =	234 mg
Fat =	5 grams
Fat % =	19 %

HUMMINGBIRD CAKE

Original Recipe:

3 cups white flour
2 cups sugar
1 tsp. salt
1 tsp. baking soda
1 tsp. cinnamon
3 whole eggs
1 ½ cups butter, melted
1 ½ tsps. vanilla
8 oz. crushed pineapple, undrained
2 mashed ripe bananas
¾ cup chopped walnuts
¾ cup chopped pecans

Alterations:

*2 cups white/1 cup pastry whole wheat
*1 cup sugar
*Omit

* ¾ cup Egg Beaters
*Half diet margarine/half nonfat yogurt

* ½ cup chopped walnuts
*Omit

Frosting:

8 oz. cream cheese
16 oz. powdered sugar
½ cup butter
1 tsp. vanilla

*1 oz. nonfat or lowfat cream cheese
*1 ½ cups powdered sugar
* ½ tsp. butter flavoring
* ½ tsp. vanilla

Directions:

COMBINE all dry ingredients and stir well. Beat egg substitute, melted margarine, and yogurt; add to dry mixture along with the vanilla, fruits, and nuts. Put batter into a nonstick or sprayed bundt cake pan. Bake at 350 for about one hour. Cool for about 10 minutes, turn out onto a serving plate and frost while still warm. 12 servings.

NOTE: The frosting will be fairly thick; it will melt and slide down the sides of the warm cake top. If the frosting is too thick add a little pineapple juice or water; if it is too thin, add a bit more powdered sugar.

Nutritional Analysis:

	Original	Lowfat Version
Kcals. =	887	371
Chol. =	157 mg	0 mg
Sodium =	579 mg	247 mg
Fat =	49 grams	9 grams
Fat % =	48 %	22 %

BLUEBERRY POPPYSEED CAKE

Original Recipe:

2/3 cup sugar
1/2 cup margarine
2 tsps. grated lemon peel
1 egg

1 1/2 cups white flour
2 Tbls. poppyseeds
1/2 tsp. baking soda
1/4 tsp. salt
1/2 cup sour cream

Alterations:

* 1/2 cup sugar or less
* 1/2 cup diet margarine

* 1/4 cup Egg Beaters *or*
    2 egg whites
*Use 1/2 cup wheat + 1 cup white

*Omit
* 1/2 cup nonfat yogurt

Filling:

2 cups fresh or frozen blueberries
    (thawed and drained)
1/3 cup sugar
2 tsps. flour
1/4 tsp. nutmeg

* 1/4 cup sugar

Glaze:

1/3 cup powdered sugar
1 tsp. milk

*1 tsp. vanilla

Directions:

HEAT oven to 350 and spray a 10-inch quiche or springform pan. In a large bowl, beat the sugar and diet margarine. Add lemon peel and egg substitute or egg whites; beat again. Combine flours, poppyseeds, and baking soda; add to creamed mixture alternately with nonfat yogurt. Spread batter over the bottom and up sides of pan.

COMBINE all filling ingredients and spoon over batter. Bake at 350 for 45 - 55 minutes or until crust is golden brown. Cool slightly and glaze with powdered sugar mixed with vanilla. Serve warm. Makes 8 servings.

Nutritional Analysis:

	Original	Lowfat Version
Kcals. =	375	293
Chol. =	33 mg	0 mg
Sodium =	272 mg	243 mg
Fat =	16 grams	7 grams
Fat % =	39 %	21 %

RHUBARB CAKE

Original Recipe:

2 cups diced rhubarb
½ cup sugar
½ cup shortening
1 ½ cups sugar
1 egg
2 cups flour
1 tsp. soda
1 tsp. salt
1 tsp. cinnamon
1 tsp. vanilla
1 cup buttermilk

Alterations:

* ⅓ to ½ cup sugar
* ½ cup diet margarine
* ½ to ¾ cup sugar
*2 egg whites
*Half whole wheat/half white

*Omit or add ⅛ tsp.

Directions:

COMBINE rhubarb and ½ cup of sugar; let stand. Mix together remaining ingredients and add rhubarb mixture. Bake at 350 in a non-stick 9X13 inch pan for 35-40 minutes. Serves 8. Delicious served warm with *Dream Whip* or nonfat frozen yogurt.

Nutritional Analysis:

	Original	Lowfat Version
Kcals. =	598	409
Chol. =	37 mg	2 mg
Sodium =	549 mg	419 mg
Fat =	19 grams	8 grams
Fat % =	28 %	18 %

BLUEBERRY BUCKLE

Original Recipe:

¾ cup sugar
½ cup shortening

1 egg
2 ½ cup flour
2 ½ tsps. baking powder
½ cup milk
2 cups blueberries

Topping:

½ cup sugar
½ tsp. cinnamon
¼ cup butter

Alterations:

* ½ cup sugar or less
* ¼ cup nonfat yogurt or cream cheese +
    ¼ cup diet margarine
*2 egg whites
*1 cup whole wheat/ 1 ½ cups white

* ½ cup nonfat milk

* ¼ cup sugar

*Use diet margarine

Directions:

CREAM sugar and diet margarine; add egg whites and beat well. Combine flour and baking powder; mix milk, flour, and egg mixture together. Fold in blueberries.

POUR batter into an 8-inch square non-stick baking pan. Mix remaining ¼ cup sugar, cinnamon, and ¼ cup diet margarine; sprinkle over batter. Bake at 375 for about 25 minutes. Serves 6.

Nutritional Analysis:	Original	Lowfat Version
Kcals. =	624	402
Chol. =	59 mg	0 mg
Sodium =	227 mg	375 mg
Fat =	27 grams	9 grams
Fat % =	38 %	20 %

SPICY APPLESAUCE CAKE

Ingredients:

1 cup white flour
1 cup whole wheat flour
2 tsps. baking powder
½ tsp. cinnamon
¼ tsp. cloves
½ cup chopped walnuts (optional)
½ cup diet margarine
½ cup honey
4 egg whites or ½ cup Egg Beaters
1 tsp. vanilla
1 ½ cups unsweetened applesauce
Spicy vanilla frosting

Spicy Vanilla Frosting:

¾ cup powdered sugar
¼ tsp. cinnamon
½ tsp vanilla
½ oz. (1 Tbls.) nonfat cream cheese

Directions:

COMBINE flours, baking powder, cinnamon, and cloves. Stir in nuts and mix well. Cream margarine and honey; add egg whites, vanilla, and applesauce. Beat well. Combine wet and dry ingredients; pour into a non-stick or sprayed 8 or 9-inch pan. Bake at 350 for about 30-45 minutes. Top of cake should spring back when touched. Frost while warm. Serves 8.

Nutritional Analysis:

Kcals. =	213
Chol. =	0 mg
Sodium =	249 mg
Fat =	6 grams
Fat % =	24 %

BASIC APPLESAUCE CAKE

Original Recipe:

2 cups flour
2 tsps. baking soda
1/2 tsp. salt
1/2 tsp. ground cloves
1/2 cup shortening
1 cup sugar
2 eggs
1 1/2 cups applesauce

Alterations:

*Use 1 cup whole wheat, 1 cup white

*Reduce to 1/8 tsp. or omit

* 1/4 cup diet margarine
* 1/2 cup sugar + 1 tsp. vanilla
*4 egg whites
*1 3/4 cups applesauce

Directions:

MIX all dry ingredients. Cream margarine, sugar, vanilla, egg whites, and applesauce. Add wet ingredients to dry and stir thoroughly. Pour batter into an 8-inch square non-stick baking pan. Bake at 350 for about 35 minutes. Makes 6 servings.

Nutritional Analysis:

	Original	Lowfat Version
Kcals. =	505	309
Chol. =	71 mg	0 mg
Sodium =	476 mg	406 mg
Fat =	19 grams	5 grams
Fat % =	34 %	12 %

QUICK FRESH FRUIT CAKE

Original Recipe:

1 *"super-moist" white cake mix*
2 *fresh peaches, sliced*
1 *cup fresh blueberries*
3/4 *cup brown sugar*
2 *tsps. cinnamon*

Alterations:

*1 Lovin Lites *white cake mix*
*2 1/2 *fresh peaches, sliced*

* 1/3 to 1/2 *cup brown sugar*

Directions:

FOLLOW instructions on the cake mix except use egg substitute or egg whites. Stir cinnamon into the mix. Pour cake mix into a 9X13 inch pan and distribute fruit evenly over the top. Sprinkle brown sugar over the top. Bake at 375 degrees for about 40 minutes or until done. Serve with vanilla frozen yogurt (about 1/2 cup per serving) and ENJOY! Makes 8 generous servings.

NOTE: Total kcalories per serving could be reduced further by simply sprinkling the top of this dessert with 2-3 tablespoons of a cinnamon and sugar mixture.

Nutritional Analysis:

	Original	Lowfat Version
Kcals. =	562	443
Chol. =	76 mg	7 mg
Sodium =	346 mg	346 mg
Fat =	15 grams	5 grams
Fat % =	25 %	11 %

OATMEAL CAKE SQUARES

Original Recipe:	Alterations:
1 ¼ cups boiling water	
1 cup raw oats	
½ cup margarine	* ½ cup diet margarine
1 cup sugar	* ½ cup sugar
1 cup brown sugar	* ½ cup brown sugar
2 eggs	*4 egg whites
1 tsp. vanilla	
2 ¼ cups flour	*Use half whole wheat flour
1 ½ tsps. cinnamon	
1 tsp. soda	
½ tsp. salt	*Omit salt
1 cup chopped nuts	* ½ cup chopped nuts or coconut
2 cups shredded carrots	
¾ cup raisins or chopped dried apricots, plumped	

Directions:

POUR boiling water over oats; cover and let stand 5-10 minutes. Beat margarine and sugars until light. Blend in egg whites and vanilla. Add oat mixture and mix well. Add the dry ingredients, stir in the carrots and raisins, and pour into a non-stick jelly roll pan. Sprinkle with nuts and bake at 350 for 20-25 minutes. Cut into 24 squares. Serves 12.

Nutritional Analysis:

	Original	Lowfat Version
Kcals. =	428	288
Chol. =	36 mg	0 mg
Sodium =	275 mg	191 mg
Fat =	15 grams	8 grams
Fat % =	31 %	23 %

TOMATO SOUP
SPICE CAKE

Original Recipe:

2 Tbls. margarine
1 cup sugar
2 cups flour
2 tsps. baking soda
1/2 tsp. cinnamon
1/2 tsp. ground ginger
1/2 tsp. allspice
1/2 tsp. nutmeg
1/2 cup raisins (optional)
1/2 cup chopped nuts (optional)
1 can condensed tomato soup

Alterations:

*Use diet margarine
* 1/2 cup sugar
*Use half whole wheat

*Use Healthy Request

Directions:

CREAM margarine and sugar. Mix the tomato soup with baking soda and add to the creamed mixture. Combine all dry ingredients and add to the soup mixture along with the raisins and nuts. Bake at 350 in a sprayed or non-stick 8-inch pan for about 30 minutes. Frost with the following cream cheese frosting when cool. Serves 6.

Frosting:

1 1/2 oz. cream cheese

*Use nonfat cream cheese
(about 2 – 3Tbls.)

1 1/2 cups powdered sugar
1 tsp. vanilla

Nutritional Analysis:

	Original	Lowfat Version	Without Nuts
Kcals. =	337	309	309
Chol. =	0 mg	0 mg	0 mg
Sodium =	342 mg	337 mg	336 mg
Fat =	8 grams	5 grams	2 grams
Fat % =	22 %	13 %	5 %

FROSTED ORANGE GINGERBREAD

Ingredients:

1 cup water
¼ cup honey
¼ cup molasses
1 Tbls. grated orange peel
½ cup orange juice
½ cup diet margarine, melted
2 egg whites or ¼ cup Egg Beaters
1 ½ cups white flour
1 cup whole wheat pastry flour
1 ½ tsps. ginger
1 tsp. baking soda
1 tsp. cinnamon
⅛ tsp. cayenne pepper
Creamy orange frosting

Creamy Orange Frosting:

¾ cup powdered sugar
½ tsp. orange flavoring
½ oz. nonfat cream cheese

Directions:

IN a large bowl, beat water, molasses, honey, orange juice, orange peel, margarine, and egg whites. Stir together flour, spices, and soda. Beat wet and dry ingredients together until smooth. Pour batter into a non-stick or sprayed 9-inch baking pan. Bake at 350 about 30 to 40 minutes. Frost with creamy orange frosting. Makes 9 servings.

Nutritional Analysis:

Kcals. =	216
Chol. =	0 mg
Sodium =	236 mg
Fat =	6 grams
Fat % =	22 %

ORANGE ALMOND
YOGURT CAKE

Original:

1 cup margarine
1 cup white sugar
2 eggs
4 egg whites
1 tsp. almond extract
2 ½ cups white flour
1 tsp. baking powder
½ tsp. salt
1 tsp. baking soda
1 cup lowfat yogurt
2 Tbls. grated orange peel
¾ cup ground almonds

Alterations:

*1 cup diet margarine

* ½ cup Egg Beaters

*1 ½ cups white/1 cup wheat

*Omit

*1 cup nonfat yogurt

*Omit

Glaze:

¼ cup white sugar
3 Tbls. orange juice
2 Tbls. lemon juice

Directions:

CREAM margarine and sugar. Add egg substitute, egg whites, and almond extract; beat well. Combine dry ingredients and add to creamed mixture alternately with yogurt. Beat until well blended. Stir in the orange peel. Pour batter into a non-stick or sprayed bundt pan. Bake in a preheated 350 oven for 50 to 60 minutes. Cool for about 10 minutes.

PREPARE GLAZE: Combine sugar, orange, and lemon juice. Heat on low; spoon glaze over cake and cool completely. Serves 12.

Nutritional Analysis:

	Original	Lowfat Version
Kcals. =	392	265
Chol. =	37 mg	0 mg
Sodium =	407 mg	332 mg
Fat =	21 grams	8 grams
Fat % =	47 %	27 %

15-MINUTE CHOCOLATE CHIP CHEESECAKE

Original:

Alterations:

Crust:

1 cup crushed chocolate sandwich cookies
3 Tbls. melted margarine

*1 cup graham cracker crumbs
*2 Tbls. melted diet margarine

Filling:

24 oz. cream cheese

*4 oz. cream cheese + 20 oz. nonfat
  cream cheese

3/4 cup sugar
3 eggs
1 cup mini-chocolate chips
1 tsp. vanilla

* 1/2 to 3/4 cup sugar
* 3/4 cup Egg Beaters
* 1/2 cup mini-chocolate chips
*2 tsps. vanilla
*1 Tbls. cornstarch

Directions:

COMBINE graham cracker crumbs and melted margarine; press onto the bottom of a 9-inch springform or pie pan. Bake 10 minutes at 350. Beat cream cheeses, sugar, *Egg Beaters*, and cornstarch; stir in chips and vanilla; pour over crust. Bake 45 minutes. Cool before removing from springform pan; refrigerate until served. Makes 12 servings.

NOTE: If ALL nonfat cream cheese is used, fat and kcals. will be further reduced. The purpose for using a small amount of regular cream cheese is to give the cheesecake a stronger flavor. The nonfat cream cheese has a very mild taste.

Nutritional Analysis:	Original	Lowfat Version	Nonfat Version
Kcals. =	500	210	183
Chol. =	115 mg	13 mg	4 mg
Sodium =	353 mg	174 mg	153 mg
Fat =	35 grams	9 grams	5 grams
Fat % =	61 %	36 %	26 %

BASIC LITE CHEESECAKE

Original Recipe:

*Graham cracker crust recipe from
    back of graham cracker box*

1 lb. cream cheese

3 eggs
½ cup sugar
⅛ tsp. vanilla

Topping:

1 pint sour cream
2 Tbls. sugar
⅛ tsp. vanilla

Alterations:

**15 graham crackers, crushed + 3 Tbls.
    diet margarine (melted)*
**16 oz. nonfat cream cheese + 2 Tbls.
    cornstarch*
* ¾ cup Egg Beaters

*1 tsp. vanilla

*8 oz. nonfat yogurt + 8 oz. Quark

* ½ tsp. vanilla

Directions:

COMBINE crushed graham crackers and melted diet margarine in a food processor. Pour crumbs into a sprayed 9 or 10-inch cheesecake pan and press firmly. Bake crust at 375 for about 8 minutes. Cool crust. Mix cream cheese, *Egg Beaters*, sugar, cornstarch, and vanilla in food processor until smooth. Pour into cooled crust and bake 20 to 25 minutes at 375. Combine yogurt, *Quark*, sugar, and vanilla; stir until smooth. Gently spread mixture over cheesecake. Return to oven for 3 minutes at 500. Makes 12 servings.

Nutritional Analysis:	Original	Lowfat Version
Kcals. =	321	146
Chol. =	111 mg	5 mg
Sodium =	235 mg	168 mg
Fat =	25 grams	3 grams
Fat % =	68 %	21 %

MAYONNAISE
CUPCAKES

Original Ingredients:

2 cups flour
2 tsps. baking soda
5 Tbls. cocoa
1 cup sugar
1 tsp. vanilla
1 cup mayonnaise
1 cup water
Frozen whipped topping

Alterations:

* 1 cup white flour + 1 cup whole
  wheat

* ½ to ¾ cup sugar
* 1 ½ tsps. vanilla
* 1 cup lowfat or nonfat mayonnaise

*Dream Whip *(prepared w/nonfat
  milk)*

Directions:

MIX dry ingredients. Combine mayonnaise, water, and vanilla. Add wet ingredients to dry ingredients; stir thoroughly. Divide batter between 24 non-stick cupcake tins and bake at 350 for about 30 minutes. When cool, cut out a small hole on the top of each cupcake (save pieces). Fill the holes with prepared *Dream Whip* and place top over whipped topping. Makes 24 small or 12 large cupcakes.

Nutritional Analysis:

	Original	Lowfat Version
Kcals. =	123	99
Chol. =	3 mg	3 mg
Sodium =	142 mg	122 mg
Fat =	5 grams	3 grams
Fat % =	33 %	28 %

RHUBARB AND DUMPLINGS

Original Recipe:

¾ cup brown sugar
¼ cup white sugar
3 Tbls. cornstarch
3 Tbls. margarine
3 cups diced rhubarb
1 ¼ cups flour
¼ cup sugar
1 ½ tsps. baking powder
¼ cup margarine
⅓ cup milk
2 tsps. sugar
¼ tsp. cinnamon

Alterations:

* ½ cup brown sugar
* ⅛ cup white sugar

*3 Tbls. diet margarine

*Use ½ cup whole wheat flour
* ⅛ to ¼ cup sugar

* ¼ cup diet margarine
*Use nonfat milk

Directions:

COMBINE 1 ¼ cups water with the brown sugar, ⅛ cup white sugar, cornstarch, and the 3 tablespoons diet margarine in a 2 quart non-stick saucepan. Add the diced rhubarb and cook until thickened over the stove. Pour thickened rhubarb into a non-stick oven-proof dish. In a bowl combine flour, remaining sugar, and baking powder. Melt the remaining margarine and add to the flour mixture along with the milk. Mix just until blended. Drop batter by rounded tablespoons onto hot rhubarb mixture. Bake in a 350 oven for about 20 minutes. Sprinkle with cinnamon sugar mixture; serve warm. Makes 8 servings.

Nutritional Analysis:

	Original	Lowfat Version
Kcals. =	318	228
Chol. =	1 mg	0 mg
Sodium =	207 mg	195 mg
Fat =	11 grams	5 grams
Fat % =	31 %	20 %

PEACH COBBLER

Original Ingredients:

6 cups sliced, peeled peaches
  (about 10 peaches)
2 eggs beaten
3 Tbls. cornstarch or flour
1 cup water
2 Tbls. butter
½ tsp. cinnamon
1 cup sugar

Alterations:

*Use unpeeled peaches or nectarines
  (peel adds fiber)
* ½ cup Egg Beaters

*2 Tbls. lowfat margarine

* ½ cup sugar

Directions:

COMBINE all of the above ingredients in a non-stick saucepan and bring to a boil, stirring frequently, until thick. Pour into a non-stick 9X13 pan.

BLEND the next 6 ingredients until smooth, then drop by spoonfuls over the fruit.

1 cup flour
1 cup sugar
1 tsp. baking powder
½ tsp. salt
3 Tbls. butter

2 eggs

*Half whole wheat/half white flour
* ½ cup sugar

*Reduce to ⅛ tsp. salt
*3 Tbls. diet margarine + 1 tsp. butter
  flavoring
* ½ cup Egg Beaters or 4 egg whites

BAKE all at 350 for 35 to 40 minutes. Serves 10.

Nutritional Analysis:

	Original	Lowfat Version
Kcals. =	324	204
Chol. =	101 mg	0 mg
Sodium =	214 mg	174 mg
Fat =	8 grams	3 grams
Fat % =	22 %	13 %

MOCK PECAN PIE

Original Recipe:

3/4 cup raw oats
3/4 cup low-sugar maple syrup
1/2 cup brown sugar
2 eggs
1 unbaked piecrust

Alterations:

* *1/2 cup* Egg Beaters
**1 unbaked lite piecrust:*
    1/2 cup white flour
    1/2 cup whole wheat flour
    1/8 tsp. salt
    3 Tbls. diet margarine
    3 Tbls. cold water

Directions:

COMBINE the oats, syrup, brown sugar, and egg substitute; pour into the unbaked 9 or 10-inch piecrust and bake at 350 for 30 to 40 minutes. This will taste like pecan pie. Makes 8 servings.

Nutritional Analysis:

	Original	Lowfat Version
Kcals. =	303	253
Chol. =	53 mg	0 mg
Sodium –	173 mg	135 mg
Fat =	9 grams	3 grams
Fat % =	27 %	10 %

BANANA CREAM PIE

Original Recipe:

1 (9-inch) baked pie shell
3 Tbls. cornstarch
1 ⅓ cups water
14 oz. sweetened condensed milk

3 egg yolks
1 tsp. vanilla
3 bananas, sliced
Lemon juice
2 Tbls. butter
Whipped cream (2 cups)

Alterations:

*Could use a "lighter" piecrust recipe
*4 Tbls. cornstarch

*14 oz. evaporated skim milk
+ ½ cup sugar
*⅜ cup Egg Beaters

*1tsp. butter flavoring
*1.3 oz. package Dream Whip made with vanilla and nonfat milk

Directions:

COMBINE: The cornstarch, water, evaporated skim milk, sugar, and egg substitute. Cook over medium heat until thickened. Remove from heat and add vanilla and butter flavoring; set aside. Dip sliced bananas in lemon juice and place on the bottom and up the sides of the pre-baked pie shell. Pour custard over bananas and chill pie thoroughly. To serve, prepare *Dream Whip* with 1 teaspoon vanilla and ½ cup nonfat milk; smooth over cooled pie. Makes 6 servings. Whipped topping is optional, of course.

Nutritional Analysis:

	Original	(no topping)	Lowfat	(no topping)
Kcals. =	626	489	383	341
Chol. =	194 mg	139 mg	3 mg	3 mg
Sodium =	320 mg	306 mg	308 mg	290 mg
Fat =	37 g	22 g	13 g	10 g
Fat % =	52 %	40 %	30 %	27 %

LEMON SOUR CREAM PIE

Original Recipe:

1 cup white sugar
3 Tbls. cornstarch
⅛ tsp. salt
1 cup whole milk
3 egg yolks
3 Tbls. butter
1 tsp. lemon peel
4 Tbls. lemon juice
1 cup sour cream
1 recipe piecrust
3 egg whites
½ tsp. cream of tartar
4 Tbls. white sugar
½ tsp. vanilla

Alterations:

*Omit
*1 cup nonfat milk
* ⅓ cup Egg Beaters
*1 Tbls. diet margarine

*1 cup nonfat yogurt

Directions:

COMBINE sugar, cornstarch, egg substitute, and cold milk in a saucepan. Cook and stir until thickened and bubbly; add diet margarine, lemon juice, and peel; cook a few minutes more. Cool until room temperature. Fold in yogurt and spoon into pie shell.

Beat egg whites with cream of tartar and vanilla to soft peaks. Gradually add sugar, beating to stiff peaks. Spread meringue atop pie, sealing to edge of pastry. Bake in oven at 350 for 10-12 minutes or until golden. Serves 8.

Nutritional Analysis: (Reduce fat further by making a lite piecrust)

	Original	Lowfat Version
Kcals. =	389	297
Chol. =	108 mg	1 mg
Sodium =	255 mg	233 mg
Fat =	21 grams	9 grams
Fat % =	47 %	28 %

BASIC LITE PUMPKIN PIE

Ingredients:

1 cup Egg Beaters
1 29 oz. can pumpkin
¾ cup sugar
¼ tsp. salt (optional)
2 tsp. cinnamon
1 tsp. ginger
½ tsp. cloves
3 cups evaporated skim milk

Directions:

BEAT all of the above ingredients until smooth; pour into prepared crusts (see below) and bake at 425 for 15 minutes. Reduce temperature to 350 and bake for about 40-50 minutes longer. Garnish with *Dream Whip* (made with nonfat milk, of course). Makes two 9-inch pies.

Crust:

1 cup whole wheat pastry flour
1 cup white flour
¼ tsp. salt
6 Tbls. diet margarine
6 Tbls. ice water

COMBINE flour, salt and diet margarine with a fork until crumbly. Add ice water and continue to mix with fork until dough holds together. Gather into a ball; divide and roll out on a lightly floured surface (use hands and additional flour minimally). Makes two single crust pies.

Nutritional Analysis: (six servings per pie):

Kcals. =	231
Chol. =	3 mg
Sodium =	272 mg
Fat =	3 grams
Fat % =	13 %

MINCEMEAT CHEESECAKE PIE

Original Recipe:

12 oz. cream cheese

2 eggs
½ cup sugar
1 Tbls. lemon peel
1 Tbls. lemon juice
2 cups mincemeat

1 single piecrust, baked
1 cup sour cream
2 Tbls. sugar
½ tsp. vanilla

Altered Version:

*12 oz. nonfat cream cheese + 2 T.
*   cornstarch*
* ½ cup Egg Beaters
* ⅓ to ½ cup sugar

*2 cups nonfat mock mincemeat (see
*   next page)*
*1 single lite piecrust, baked
*1 cup nonfat yogurt + 1 Tbls. cornstarch

Directions:

BEAT cream cheese, *Egg Beaters*, sugar, cornstarch, lemon peel, and juice until very smooth. Put two cups of mincemeat into a baked 9-inch lite piecrust. Pour cream cheese mixture over mincemeat and bake at 375 for 20 minutes.

Mix the yogurt, sugar, vanilla, and cornstarch and spread over top of baked pie; return to oven for 10 minutes. Serves 6 - 8.

Nutritional Analysis:

	Original	Lowfat version
Kcals. =	699	448
Chol. =	150 mg	2 mg
Sodium =	421 mg	215 mg
Fat =	40 grams	6 grams
Fat % =	50 %	11 %

MOM'S MOCK MINCEMEAT

Ingredients:

2 cups chopped green tomatoes
2 ½ cups raisins
2 cups peeled, chopped apples (half Golden Delicious)
¾ cup sugar
⅓ cup apple cider vinegar
1 Tbls. orange juice concentrate
1 cup water
1 Tbls. lemon juice
1 ½ tsp. cinnamon
¾ tsp. each ground cloves and allspice
½ tsp. nutmeg
1 tsp. brandy flavoring or 1 Tbls. brandy

Directions:

MIX all ingredients (except brandy flavoring or brandy) and cook over low heat, stirring often, until thick. Add flavoring and cook 5-10 minutes longer. Put into a sterilized glass quart jar and seal with a sterile cap and ring OR put into an airtight container in refrigerator. Keeps for at least a year if a sterilized jar is used. Enough for one mincemeat pie or 8 servings.

Nutritional Analysis:

Kcals. =	263
Chol. =	0 mg
Sodium =	12 mg
Fat =	1 gram
Fat % =	2 %

FRESH FRUIT TART

Original Recipe:

1 ¼ cup white flour

½ tsp. salt

½ tsp. sugar
½ cup butter
¼ cup ice water

Alterations:

* ¾ cup white flour + ¾ cup whole wheat flour
* Omit salt and add ½ tsp. baking powder

* ½ cup diet margarine

Directions:

DO NOT MAKE TART SHELL IN THE FOOD PROCESSOR. Combine flours, baking powder and sugar in a small bowl; cut in diet margarine and combine with enough ice water to form a ball of dough (use hands minimally). Roll out pastry and place in a tart pan. Poke dough with a fork and bake at 375 for about 15 minutes. Set aside.

Filling:

8 oz. cream cheese
2 Tbls. lemon juice
1 cup white sugar
1 cup sliced strawberries
1 cup grapes or kiwi
1 Tbls. melted preserves

*8 oz. nonfat cream cheese or Quark
* ½ tsp. lemon extract
* ½ to 1 cup white sugar

Directions:

CREAM the *Quark* or nonfat cream cheese, lemon extract, and sugar; spread evenly over the bottom of the tart shell. Decorate tart with fresh fruit and glaze with preserves. Chill and serve. Makes 8 servings.

Nutritional Analysis:

	Original	Lowfat Version
Kcals. =	396	308
Chol. =	62 mg	5 mg
Sodium =	316 mg	243 mg
Fat =	22 grams	6 grams
Fat % =	48 %	26 %

RHUBARB CRUNCH

Original Recipe:

Crumb Topping:

1 cup flour
¾ cup rolled oats
1 cup brown sugar
½ cup melted butter
1 tsp. cinnamon

Sauce Mixture:

4 cups diced rhubarb
1 cup sugar
2 Tbls. cornstarch
1 cup water
1 tsp. vanilla

Alterations:

*Half whole wheat/half white
*1 ¼ cup oats
* ½ cup brown sugar
* ½ cup diet margarine

* ½ to ¾ cup sugar

Directions:

MIX together crumb topping ingredients until crumbly. Press half of the crumbs in a non-stick 9-inch pan; cover with rhubarb. In a small saucepan combine the sugar, cornstarch, water, and vanilla. Cook stirring until thick and clear. Pour over rhubarb. Top with remaining crumbs. Bake in a 350 oven for 1 hour (325 for glass dish). 8 servings.

Nutritional Analysis:	Original	Lowfat Version
Kcals. =	405	321
Chol. =	31 mg	0 mg
Sodium =	147 mg	114 mg
Fat =	12 grams	7 grams
Fat % =	27 %	18 %

CHERRY TORTE

Original Recipe:

1 cup white flour
½ cup butter
5 Tbls. powdered sugar
1 cup sweet pie cherries
2 whole eggs
1 ½ cups sugar

½ tsp. salt
¾ tsp. baking powder

Alterations:

*Half white/half wheat
* ½ cup diet margarine
*4 Tbls. powdered sugar

* ½ cup Egg Beaters
* ½ - ¾ cup sugar + ½ Tbls.
    cornstarch
*Omit salt

*1 tsp. vanilla

Directions:

COMBINE flours, powdered sugar, and diet margarine. Press dough into an 8-inch non-stick pan. Top dough with cherries. Beat egg substitute, cornstarch, sugar, baking powder, and vanilla; pour over cherries. Bake at 350 for about 30-45 minutes. Delicious served warm. Serves 6.

Nutritional Analysis:

	Original	Lowfat Version
Kcals. =	467	283
Chol. =	112 mg	0 mg
Sodium =	370 mg	261 mg
Fat =	17 grams	8 grams
Fat % =	33 %	24 %

ELEGANT DESSERT

Original Recipe:

1 cup flour
2 Tbls. sugar
½ cup margarine
1 cup chopped almonds

Filling:

8 oz. cream cheese
12 oz. Cool Whip

2 packages instant pudding
  (chocolate or pistachio)
2 ½ cups milk

Alterations:

*Half whole wheat flour

* ¼ cup diet margarine
* ⅓ cup chopped almonds

*8 oz. nonfat cream cheese
*1 package Dream Whip *prepared with*
  nonfat milk and vanilla

*2 ½ cups nonfat milk

Directions:

COMBINE crust ingredients and press into 9X13 non-stick pan. Bake at 325 until lightly brown. Cool completely. Mix the nonfat cream cheese with half of the *Dream Whip*. Spread over crust. Prepare the pudding mix with 2 ½ cups of nonfat milk and spread over the cream cheese. Top with remaining *Dream Whip* (sprinkle with a few sliced almonds, if desired). Serves 10.

Nutritional Analysis:

	Original	Lowfat Version
Kcals. =	494	226
Chol. =	33 mg	9 mg
Sodium =	448 mg	350 mg
Fat =	35 grams	8 grams
Fat % =	62 %	32 %

SWEET CHERRITY PIE

Original Recipe:

1 cup flour
½ to 1 cup chopped nuts
¼ cup brown sugar
½ cup soft margarine

Filling:

8 oz. cream cheese
½ tsp. almond extract
1 cup powdered sugar
21 oz. canned cherry pie filling
*1 cup whipping cream, whipped
    & sweetened*

Alterations:

*Half wheat flour
* ⅓ cup chopped nuts

* ⅓ cup diet margarine

*8 oz. nonfat cream cheese

**1 package Dream Whip prepared
    with skim milk and vanilla*

Directions:

PREHEAT oven to 375. In a 9X13 non-stick pan, combine the first four ingredients. Bake 15-20 minutes until golden brown; stir once while baking. Reserve ½ cup crumbs for top. Using a spoon, firmly press remaining warm crumb mixture into a non-stick 9 or 10-inch pie plate. Chill crust.

IN a medium bowl, blend the cream cheese, powdered sugar, and almond extract. Spread over crust. Fold pie filling into prepared whipped topping and spoon over cream cheese layer. Sprinkle with reserved crumb mixture. Chill 1- 2 hours before serving. Store in the refrigerator. Serves 8.

Nutritional Analysis:	Original	Lowfat Version
Kcals. =	553	327
Chol. =	72 mg	1 mg
Sodium =	255 mg	154 mg
Fat =	37 grams	10 grams
Fat % =	59 %	26 %

FRENCH STRAWBERRY PIE

Original Recipe:
1 baked pastry shell
4 cups fresh strawberries
3 oz. cream cheese
½ cup water
½ cup sugar
3 Tbls. cornstarch
1 cup Cool Whip

Alterations:
*Lite pastry shell (see next page)

*Nonfat cream cheese

*1 cup prepared Dream Whip *(use nonfat milk)*

Directions:
SPREAD nonfat cream cheese over bottom of pastry. Cover with half of the berries. Mash the remaining berries and combine with water, sugar, and cornstarch. Cook mashed berries until thickened. Cool and pour into baked shell. Chill overnight. Serve with prepared *Dream Whip*. Makes 8 servings.

Nutritional Analysis:

	Original	Lowfat Version
Kcals. =	247	182
Chol. =	13 mg	0 mg
Sodium =	178 mg	70 mg
Fat =	13 grams	4 grams
Fat % =	45 %	19 %

GERMAN CHOCOLATE PIE

Original Recipe:

1 baked pie crust

Alterations:

* ½ cup white flour
  ½ cup pastry wheat flour
  ⅛ tsp. salt
  3 Tbls. diet margarine
  3 - 4 Tbls. cold water

Filling:

½ cup sugar
½ cup Watkins Coconut Dessert Mix
1 Tbls. flour
2 ½ cups whole milk

4 eggs, divided
4 oz. sweet cooking chocolate
1 tsp. vanilla
⅔ cup chopped pecans

* ¼ cup coconut
* ¼ cup cornstarch
*1 ½ cups nonfat milk + 1 cup
  evaporated skim milk
*1 cup Egg Beaters
* ¼ - ⅓ cup cocoa powder

* ⅓ cup pecans or walnuts

Meringue:

4 egg whites
¼ tsp. cream of tartar
½ cup super fine sugar

* ¼ to ⅓ cup sugar

Directions:

PREPARE pie shell; bake for 10-15 minutes and set aside. In a medium non-stick saucepan, combine ½ cup sugar, cornstarch, cocoa powder, and coconut. Mix the milk and the egg substitute; add to the sugar mixture. Cook over medium heat, stirring constantly until mixture thickens and comes to a full boil. Remove from heat; add vanilla and all but 1 tablespoon of nuts to thickened mixture. Pour into baked pie shell.

COMBINE the 4 egg whites and cream of tartar in a small mixing bowl. Beat until soft peaks form. Gradually add the sugar, 1 tablespoon at a time, beating until stiff peaks form. Spoon meringue carefully over hot pie filling. Seal meringue to rim of pie shell. Sprinkle with remaining nuts and bake at 400 for about 5-10 minutes. Cool 2 hours. Refrigerate pie until ready to serve. Refrigerate leftover pie. Makes 8 servings.

Continued on next page

German Chocolate Pie - Continued

Nutritional Analysis:	Original	Lowfat Version
Kcals. =	510	339
Chol. =	118 mg	2 mg
Sodium =	312 mg	216 mg
Fat =	26 grams	7 grams
Fat % =	44 %	19 %

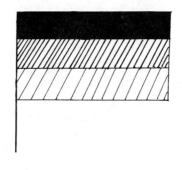

APPLE TORTE

Original Recipe:

2 cups raw apple, grated
1 cup sugar
1 beaten egg
4 Tbls. shortening
1 cup flour
1 tsp. cinnamon
½ tsp. salt
1 tsp. soda
½ cup chopped nuts
½ cup brown sugar

Alterations:

* ¼ - ½ cup sugar
*2 egg whites or ½ cup Egg Beaters
*4 Tbls. diet margarine
*Use half whole wheat flour

*Omit salt and add 1 tsp. vanilla

* ¼ cup chopped nuts
* ¼ cup brown sugar

Directions:

COMBINE the grated apple and sugar. Beat in the egg whites and diet margarine. Add dry ingredients and nuts. Spread into a non-stick 8X8 inch pan. Sprinkle with brown sugar. Bake at 325 for about 45 minutes. Serves 6.

Nutritional Analysis:

	Original	Lowfat Version
Kcals. =	447	267
Chol. =	36 mg	0 mg
Sodium =	335 mg	252 mg
Fat =	16 grams	7 grams
Fat % =	31 %	23 %

CREAM CHEESE CLOUDS

Original Recipe:

8 oz. cream cheese
½ cup powdered sugar
¼ tsp. vanilla
1 cup heavy whipping cream
1 can cherry pie filling
Chopped nuts (optional)

Alterations:

*Use lowfat or nonfat cream cheese
* ¼ to ½ cup powdered sugar

*1 package Dream Whip *(1.3 oz.)*
*Or make a fresh fruit filling
*Omit

Directions:

MIX cream cheese, sugar, and vanilla at medium speed on electric mixer. Prepare packaged *Dream Whip* with ½ cup skim milk and ½ tsp. vanilla. Whip until thickened; add cream cheese mixture and continue to beat well. Using the back of a spoon, shape whipped mixture into 10 (3 ½ inch) shells. Place on waxed paper lined cookie sheet. Freeze 2 hours or overnight. When ready to serve, fill with cherry pie filling or thickened fresh fruit filling. Serves 10.

Nutritional Analysis:

	Original	Lowfat Cr. Cheese	Nonfat Cr. Cheese
Kcals. =	267	168	129
Chol. =	57 mg	17 mg	2 mg
Sodium =	78 mg	57 mg	29 mg
Fat =	18 grams	7 grams	2 grams
Fat % =	60 %	35 %	13 %

FOUR LAYER CHOCOLATE DELIGHT

Original Recipe: Alterations:

Layer #1 -
1 cup flour   **Use half whole wheat flour*
½ cup chopped nuts   ** ¼ chopped nuts*
½ cup margarine   ** ¼ cup diet margarine*

Layer #2
1 cup Cool Whip   **1 cup* Dream Whip *made with nonfat milk*

1 cup powdered sugar
8 oz. cream cheese   **Use nonfat cream cheese*

Layer #3
2 small packages chocolate
*   instant pudding*
3 cups cold milk   **Use nonfat milk*

Layer #4
1 cup Cool Whip   **1 cup* Dream Whip *made with nonfat milk*

¼ cup chopped nuts   **2 Tbls. chopped nuts*

Directions:

COMBINE Layer #1 ingredients and press into a 9X13 inch non-stick pan. Bake at 375 for 20 minutes. Cool and set aside. Combine 1 cup prepared *Dream Whip*, powdered sugar, and cream cheese; mix until fluffy. Spread on cooled Layer #1. Mix pudding and milk and spread on Layer #2. Top all with remaining *Dream Whip* and sprinkle with nuts. Chill until served. Serves 12.

Nutritional Analysis:	Original	Lowfat Version
Kcals. =	385	247
Chol. =	28 mg	9 mg
Sodium =	370 mg	292 mg
Fat =	24 grams	8 grams
Fat % =	55 %	28 %

CHERRY CHEESE DESSERT

Original Recipe:	Alterations:

Crust:

1 cup margarine	* *½ cup diet margarine*
2 cups flour	**Use half whole wheat flour*
1 Tbls. sugar	

Filling:

2 cups Dream Whip	**2 cups prepared* Dream Whip
8 oz. cream cheese	**Use nonfat cream cheese OR half lite / half nonfat cream cheese*
1 cup powdered sugar	
1 can cherry pie filling	**Or 1 can sweet cherries, sweetened slightly and thickened with cornstarch*

Directions:

MIX crust ingredients and press into a 9X13 inch non-stick pan. Bake at 350 for 15 - 20 minutes. Cool. Mix prepared *Dream Whip* (made with nonfat milk) with the powdered sugar and cream cheese. Spread over crust and refrigerate 1 hour. Top with cherries. Serves 10.

Nutritional Analysis:	Original	Lowfat Version
Kcals. =	511	276
Chol. =	25 mg	2 mg
Sodium =	287 mg	138 mg
Fat =	30 grams	7 grams
Fat % =	52 %	21 %

CHOCOLATE STRAWBERRY SHORTCAKE

Original Recipe:

6 cups fresh strawberries
1 ⅔ cups flour
⅓ cup cocoa powder
½ cup sugar
1 Tbls. baking powder
¼ tsp. salt
1 egg
½ cup butter
⅔ cup milk
1 cup heavy cream

2 Tbls. sugar

Alterations:

* *⅔ cup whole wheat + 1 cup white*

* *¼ cup + 2 Tbls. sugar*

*Omit
2 egg whites or ¼ cup Egg Beaters
* *¼ cup diet margarine*
1 cup nonfat milk + 1 tsp. vanilla
2 cups Dream Whip *prepared with nonfat milk*

Directions:

SLICE berries and sprinkle with the 2 tablespoons sugar; set aside. For shortcake, combine flour, cocoa, remaining sugar, and baking powder. Cut in the diet margarine. Combine egg whites, vanilla, and milk; add all at once to dry ingredients. Stir just until moistened. Spread dough in a non-stick 8-inch round baking pan. Bake at 450 for 15-18 minutes. Serve shortcake warm with berries and whipped topping. Makes 8 servings.

Nutritional Analysis:

	Original	Lowfat Version
Kcals. =	401	237
Chol. =	101 mg	3 mg
Sodium =	318 mg	237 mg
Fat =	25 grams	7 grams
Fat % =	55 %	24 %

STRAWBERRY TIRAMISU

Original Recipe:

12 oz. light cream cheese

¾ cup powdered sugar
7 Tbls. Marsala wine
½ cup sour cream
1 pint fresh strawberries
¾ cup boiling water
2 Tbls. sugar
2 ½ tsps. instant espresso or coffee powder
2 ¼ packages ladyfingers
1 oz. semisweet chocolate, grated

Alterations:

*4 oz. cream cheese + 8 oz. nonfat cream cheese

* ½ cup lowfat or nonfat yogurt

Directions:

BLEND cream cheese, powdered sugar, and 5 tablespoons Marsala wine in processor until smooth. Mix in yogurt. Slice all of the strawberries in half. Combine boiling water, 2 tablespoons sugar and espresso powder in a medium bowl; stir to dissolve. Mix in remaining Marsala wine. Dip ladyfingers into espresso, one at a time, and place enough to cover the bottom, flat side up, of an 8-inch square dish with 2 inch sides. Spread ⅔ cream cheese mixture over ladyfingers and cover with half of the sliced strawberries. Repeat layer, ending with remaining cream cheese. Sprinkle with grated chocolate. Arrange remaining halved strawberries around edge of pan. Cover and refrigerate until set, at least 4 hours. Cut into 6 squares.

Nutritional Analysis:

	Original	Lowfat Version
Kcals. =	449	366
Chol. =	184 mg	157 mg
Sodium =	182 mg	142 mg
Fat =	23 grams	13 grams
Fat % =	47 %	33 %

PINEAPPLE CHEESE
BREAD PUDDING

Original Recipe:

4 slices white or whole wheat bread
1 cup crushed pineapple
2 eggs
½ cup part-skim Ricotta cheese
2 tsps. vanilla
1 tsp. lemon extract
½ tsp. cinnamon
2 cups nonfat milk
8 tsp. sugar

Alterations:

*Use whole wheat or cracked wheat

*4 egg whites or ½ cup Egg Beaters
*Use nonfat or lowfat Ricotta

*4-6 tsp. sugar

Directions:

PREHEAT oven to 350. Place bread cubes in an 8-inch square non-stick or sprayed pan. Spread pineapple evenly over the bread. In a blender or processor, combine remaining ingredients. Blend until smooth. Pour mixture evenly over bread and pineapple. Let stand 5 minutes. Sprinkle with additional cinnamon, if desired. Bake uncovered, 35-40 minutes, until set. Chill and cut into squares or serve warm. 4 servings.

Nutritional Analysis:

	Original	Altered Version
Kcals. =	254	219
Chol. –	118 mg	8 mg
Sodium =	239 mg	251 mg
Fat =	6 grams	3 grams
Fat % =	21 %	11 %

CREAMY RICE PUDDING

Original Recipe:
1 ½ cups cooked white rice
2 cups whole milk

⅓ cup sugar
¼ tsp. salt
1 whole egg
⅔ cup raisins
1 Tbls. butter
½ tsp. vanilla
¼ tsp. nutmeg
¼ tsp. cinnamon

Alterations:
*Half white/half brown rice
*1 cup evaporated skim milk +
    1 cup nonfat milk

* ⅛ tsp. salt or omit
* ¼ cup Egg Beaters + 1 Tbls. cornstarch

*1 Tbls. diet margarine

Directions:

COMBINE rice, 1 ½ cups milk, and sugar in a non-stick saucepan. Cook over medium heat, stirring occasionally, 15-20 minutes. Blend remaining ½ cup milk, cornstarch, and egg substitute. Stir into rice mixture. Add raisins and cook 2 minutes longer, stirring constantly. Add diet margarine and vanilla. Spoon into serving dishes. Sprinkle with nutmeg and cinnamon. Makes 4 servings.

Nutritional Analysis:

	Original	Lowfat Version
Kcals. =	365	354
Chol. =	78 mg	4 mg
Sodium =	238 mg	307 mg
Fat =	9 grams	4 grams
Fat % =	21 %	9 %

SOUTHERN BREAD PUDDING

Original Recipe:
6 slices of bread (buttered, toasted, diced)
3 whole eggs, beaten
8 Tbls. sugar
1 #2 can fruit cocktail, drained
1/4 cup raisins
1 qt. milk, scalded

1 tsp. vanilla

2 Tbls. melted butter

Alterations:
*6 slices diced wheat bread
* 3/4 cups Egg Beaters
*4 Tbls. sugar

*2 cups nonfat milk + 2 cups
    evaporated skim milk
*1 tsp. vanilla + 1 tsp. butter
    and/or rum flavoring
*Omit

Directions:

SOAK bread cubes in 1 cup of hot milk; in a separate bowl, combine the egg substitute, sugar, fruit cocktail, and raisins. Pour the remaining 3 cups of hot milk slowly over the egg mixture, stirring rapidly. Add the bread cubes, butter flavoring, and vanilla and mix well. Bake for 45 minutes at 350 in a non-stick or sprayed 2 quart casserole dish. When pudding is done, top with meringue and bake at 425 for 5 minutes. Serves 6.

Meringue:
4 egg whites + 1/4 tsp. cream of tartar + 3 Tbls. sugar (beat until stiff peaks form).

Nutritional Analysis:	Original	Lowfat Version
Kcals. =	411	319
Chol. =	149 mg	5 mg
Sodium =	360 mg	342 mg
Fat =	17 grams	1 gram
Fat % =	36 %	3 %

LAURIE'S LITE PLUM PUDDING

Ingredients:

30 oz. canned plums
2 tsps. baking soda
¼ cup diet margarine
½ to 1 cup white sugar
4 egg whites or ½ cup Egg Beaters
1 tsp. lemon juice
2 tsps. vanilla
2 Tbls. brandy OR milk + brandy flavoring
1 ¼ cups white flour (or mix with some whole wheat)
1 tsp. cinnamon
¼ tsp. salt or omit
1 cup raisins, plumped
¼ to ½ cup walnuts or omit

Directions:

DRAIN and remove pits from plums; puree (should equal 1 cup). Stir in soda; set aside. Cream margarine and sugar; add egg whites, lemon juice, vanilla, brandy, and plum puree. Combine flour, cinnamon, and salt; add to creamed mixture and stir well. Add raisins and nuts.

SPRAY a mold or 2 lb. coffee can; pour in plum pudding and cover container tightly with heavy aluminum foil. Place container in a deep kettle on a rack and pour in boiling water until it comes up to (but not touching) the bottom of the mold. Cover kettle and keep water boiling gently while the pudding cooks. If necessary, add more boiling water during cooking. Steam for 2 - 2 ½ hours. Cool 10 minutes and unmold. Serve; or cool, wrap and store. Makes about 8 servings. Pudding is best served warm. Serve with *Dream Whip* (prepared with nonfat milk).

Nutritional Analysis:

	w/diet marg.	w/o nuts
	1/2 cup sugar	w /diet marg
Kcals. =	282	234
Chol. =	0 mg	0 mg
Sodium =	372 mg	372 mg
Fat =	8 grams	3 grams
Fat % =	23 %	12 %

NUT- BUTTER FANTASY FUDGE

Original Recipe:

3 cups white sugar
¾ cup margarine

⅔ cup evaporated milk

12 oz. chocolate chips
7 oz. marshmallow cream
1 tsp. vanilla

1 cup chopped nuts

Alterations:

*2 Tbls. Adams creamy peanut butter
  (or almond butter, hazelnut butter,
  etc.)
* ⅔ cup evaporated skim milk or nonfat
  cream cheese
*6 oz. chocolate chips

*Or other companion flavoring such as
  almond extract
*Omit nuts
*6 Tbls. cornstarch

Directions:

COMBINE sugar, cornstarch, peanut butter, and evaporated skim milk in a non-stick saucepan; boil for five minutes. Remove from heat and add chocolate chips, vanilla, and marshmallow cream. Stir until smooth and spread quickly into a non-stick 9X13 inch pan. Cool completely and cut into about 48 (1 ounce) squares. This fudge should be wrapped in foil and stored in the freezer to prevent it from drying out (and from eating too much of it!).

Nutritional Analysis : (per piece)	Original	Lowfat Version
Kcals. =	143	87
Chol. =	1 mg	0 mg
Sodium =	41 mg	7 mg
Fat =	7 grams	1.6 grams
Fat % =	43 %	16 %

Snacks, Sauces &
Side Dishes

—

•

*Basic Recipe Alteration Techniques
for Snacks, Sauces & Side Dishes*

•

Snacks

•

Sauces

•

Side Dishes

Basic Recipe Alteration Techniques

•

Snacks, Sauces & Side Dishes

Snacks:

FOLLOW the same principles outlined in the previous sections AND:

1. Nonfat refried beans are now available in the can. If you prefer to make your own, simply puree drained pinto beans in the food processor with some salsa for flavor. Making your own will reduce sodium.

2. To make chips simply cut thin corn tortillas in triangles and bake in a single layer on a non-stick cookie sheet at 350 for about 15 minutes (or until crisp). If you are in a hurry, tortillas can also be baked whole and simply broken into pieces. One of the only nonfat commercially produced tortilla chips on the market at this time is *The Guiltless Gourmet* brand. Unfortunately, they are not available in all stores.

3. All packaged spice mixes (taco, gravy, dressings, stew, spaghetti, etc.) are extremely high in sodium. Make you own spice blends or purchase *Mrs. Dash's* brand.

4. Low-sodium sauces such as, Worcestershire, soy, and teriyaki are available everywhere and should always be selected.

5. It is almost impossible to reduce the fat in some dips and spreads to below 30% of total kcalories. However, when accompanied by nonfat chips, fresh vegetables and fruits, and breads, they can become reasonably low-in-fat in the quantities usually consumed. NOTE: If you are serving a complete meal for guests, it is best to prepare very lowfat appetizers (such as fresh vegetables and dip) or offer a warm beverage instead. P.S. There are also times when appetizers are the only foods served at gatherings. In that sense, they become the main dish for most people and should be more substantial (especially when alcohol is being served).

Sauces:

FOLLOW the same principles outlined in the previous sections AND:

1. Homemade syrups and sauces can be made without added fat by using cornstarch as a thickening agent.

2. Always use lowfat margarine and cheeses, and skim or evaporated skim milk for cream type sauces.

3. Herbs, spices, and flavorings should be used liberally to add flavor and color to low-fat sauces.

4. When a sauce calls for egg yolks, use egg substitute equal to ⅛ cup per yolk.

Side Dishes:

FOLLOW the same principles outlined in the previous sections AND:

1. If you are serving a 3-4 ounce portion of lean meat, fish, or poultry as part of a dinner entree, side dishes should be kept as lowfat as possible due to the naturally occurring fat in all animal products. However, cooking for guests and special occasions are exceptions to that rule. Still, the basic healthy food preparation principles outlined in this cookbook should be followed even when preparing more elaborate side dishes.

2. When a recipe calls for sausage, make it yourself from lean ground turkey. When you think about what sausage is made out of, ground pork plus spices, this technique makes a great deal of common sense.

Spices for Italian sausage = (per 1 lb. ground turkey)

1 – 2 tsps. anise seed
2 tsps. fennel seed
1 – 2 tsp. thyme
⅛ tsp. crushed red pepper
⅛ tsp. garlic powder
⅛ tsp. salt (optional)

Spices for breakfast sausage = (per 1 lb. ground turkey)

2 tsp. thyme
2 tsp. sage or poultry seasoning
⅛ tsp. each pepper and salt
1 tsp. anise seed
⅛ tsp. onion powder

Note:

Ground turkey should be mixed thoroughly with the spices early in the day or the day before to allow the spice flavors to permeate the meat. To cook, brown the meat in a covered non-stick pan.

CREAMY ORANGE FRAPPE

Original Recipe:

⅓ cup frozen orange juice concentrate
½ cup whole milk

½ cup water
½ tsp. vanilla
¼ cup sugar
5 - 6 ice cubes

Alterations:

* ½ cup evaporated skim milk or
½ cup nonfat milk

*2 Tbls. sugar

Directions:

BLEND all but the ice cubes in a blender or food processor. Add cubes one at a time until the last one is dissolved. Serves 4.

Nutritional Analysis:

	Original	Altered Version
Kcals. =	417	345
Sodium =	21 mg	42 mg
Fat =	1 gram	0 gram
Fat % =	9 %	1 %

STRAWBERRY – MELON SHAKE

Original Recipe:

3 cups vanilla ice cream
12 tsps. sugar
6 cups honeydew melon
    chunks, chilled
3 cups frozen strawberries

Alterations:

*3 cups lowfat frozen vanilla yogurt
*6 - 12 tsps. sugar

Directions:

BLEND or process all ingredients thoroughly. Serve immediately. Makes 12 servings.

Nutritional Analysis:

	Original	Lowfat Version
Kcals. =	125	104
Chol. =	15 mg	4 mg
Sodium =	38 mg	32 mg
Fat –	4 grams	1 gram
Fat % =	26 %	10 %

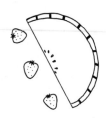

BEAN DIP

Original Recipe:

2 cans refried beans (16 oz. each)
16 oz. Italian stewed tomatoes
1 small can diced green chilies
1/4 cup sauted onions
1/2 cup salsa
4 oz. shredded cheddar cheese

Alterations:

*Use nonfat refried beans
*Use no-salt stewed tomatoes + seasonings

*Saute in non-stick pan

*Use lowfat cheddar

Directions:

MIX first 5 ingredients together in a non-stick pan. Heat on medium-low heat until hot. Stir in cheese and heat until cheese is melted. Serve warm with nonfat chips. Serves 8.

Nutritional Analysis:	Original	Altered Version
Kcals. =	235	259
Chol. =	15 mg	10 mg
Sodium =	713 mg	84 mg
Fat =	6 grams	4 grams
Fat % =	27 %	14 %

NOTE: To make chips simply cut thin corn tortillas in triangles and bake in a single layer on a non-stick cookie sheet at 350 for about 15 minutes (or until crisp). One of the only nonfat commercially produced tortilla chips on the market at this time is *The Guiltless Gourmet* brand. Unfortunately, they are not easy to find.

NACHO DIP

Original Recipe:
1 can (14.5 oz.) refried beans
16 oz. lean ground beef

1 package taco spice mix

3-4 cups shredded cheddar cheese

1 large tomato, chopped
8 oz. sour cream

1 can sliced black olives
1 cup salsa

Alterations:
*28 oz. nonfat refried beans, warmed
*4 oz. ground turkey + 1/2 cup chopped
     onion
*1 Tbls. chili powder, 1 tsp. cumin,
     1 tsp. oregano, 1 tsp. cilantro
*1 1/3 cups shredded lowfat cheddar
     cheese

*4 oz. nonfat Quark + 4 oz. nonfat
     yogurt
*Omit olives
*1 1/2 cups salsa

Directions:
BROWN the lean ground turkey, onion, and spices; add 1/2 cup of salsa. On a platter, spread the warm beans and 1/2 cup cheese. Cover with the meat mixture and 1/2 cup cheese. Top with remaining cup of salsa and the *Quark*/yogurt mixture. Layer with the chopped tomato and remaining cheese. Serve with baked crisp corn tortilla pieces. Serves 10 (as an appetizer).

Nutritional Analysis:	Original	Lowfat Version
Kcals. =	434	191
Chol. =	89 mg	21 mg
Sodium =	1014 mg	634 mg
Fat =	30 grams	7 grams
Fat % =	63 %	31 %

MUSTARD DIP

Original Recipe:

1 cup mayonnaise
1 cup milk
1 Tbls. yellow mustard
1 Tbls. sugar
Sliced zucchini, cauliflower, celery, broccoli and carrots

Alterations:

*1 cup nonfat mayonnaise
*3/4 to 1 cup nonfat milk or buttermilk

Directions:

COMBINE all dip ingredients and chill until ready to serve. Serve with assorted sliced fresh vegetables. Makes 16 one ounce servings.

Nutritional Analysis:

	Original	Lowfat Version
Kcals. =	112	17
Chol. =	10 mg	.5 mg
Sodium =	98 mg	98 mg
Fat =	12 grams	0 grams
Fat % =	91 %	5 %

NIPPY BLUE CHEESE DIP

Original Recipe:

6 oz. cream cheese, softened
3 Tbls. milk
1 Tbls. mayonnaise
1/2 tsp. Worcestershire sauce
1/4 cup crumbled blue cheese

Alterations:

*Use nonfat cream cheese
*Use nonfat milk
*Use nonfat mayonnaise
*Use low-sodium Worcestershire
* 1/8 - 1/4 cup blue cheese

Directions:

BLEND cream cheese, milk, mayonnaise, and Worcestershire sauce; fold in blue cheese. Serve with cut-up assorted vegetables or apple slices. Makes 8 appetizer servings.

Nutritional Analysis:

	Original	Lowfat Version
Kcals. =	115	40
Chol. =	30 mg	6 mg
Sodium =	196 mg	130 mg
Fat =	11 grams	2 grams
Fat % =	85 %	47 %

NOTE: Using only 1/8 cup of blue cheese will reduce fat to 1 gram (35 %) per serving. Sodium would drop to 81 mg., Chol. to 3 mg, and total Kcals. to 28 per serving.

FONDUE

Original Recipe:

1 clove garlic
1 ½ cups dry white wine

1 Tbls. lemon juice
1 lb. Swiss cheese, shredded
3 Tbls. white flour
Pepper and nutmeg to taste
2 loaves French bread, cubed

Alterations:

*Or minced dried garlic
*1 cup dry white wine + ½ cup
  skim milk

*8 oz. lite Swiss cheese, shredded
*1 - 2 Tbls. cornstarch

Directions:

RUB THE INSIDE of a non-stick pan with the cut clove of garlic or add dried minced garlic to the pan. Pour the wine into the pan and heat but do not boil. When wine is hot add lemon juice. Combine the milk (you could also use evaporated skim milk) with the cornstarch and add gradually to the hot wine mixture. Stir constantly while adding the shredded cheese gradually. Stir until thickened and creamy. Add pepper and nutmeg to taste; bring just to a boil. Serve hot with bread cubes for dunking. 4 main dish servings or 12 snack servings.

Nutritional Analysis:

	Original	Lowfat Version
Kcals. =	913	642
Chol. =	104 mg	39 mg
Sodium =	1112 mg	942 mg
Fat =	37 grams	18 grams
Fat % =	36 %	24 %

HUMMUS

Original Recipe:
2 cloves garlic, minced
2 cups canned garbanzo beans, drained
1/3 cup tahini
1/3 cup lemon juice
1/2 cup water
3 Tbls. olive oil
1/4 tsp. cayenne pepper

Alterations:

*2 Tbls. tahini
*3 Tbls. lemon juice
* 1/2 cup chicken broth
*Omit olive oil

Directions:

PUREE beans and combine with all other ingredients. Serve with pita bread wedges. Serving size is 1 tablespoon.

Nutritional Analysis:

	Original	Lowfat Version
Kcals. =	35	19
Chol. =	0 mg	0 mg
Sodium =	1 mg	10 mg
Fat =	2.4 grams	.7 grams
Fat % =	57 %	30 %

CHEDDAR SPREAD

Original Recipe:

1 1/2 cups shredded cheddar cheese
3 oz. cream cheese
1/4 cup butter
1/3 cup milk
1 Tbls. chopped green onion
1/2 tsp. Dijon mustard
1/4 tsp. Worcestershire sauce
A few drops of hot pepper sauce
Serve with crackers

Alterations:

*Use lowfat cheddar
*Use nonfat cream cheese
*Use diet margarine
*Use nonfat milk

*Use low-sodium Worcestershire

*Serve with bagels, lowfat saltines, or
wheat rolls

Directions:

BRING cheeses and margarine to room temperature and combine with an electric mixer. Add milk, green onion, mustard, Worcestershire sauce, and hot pepper sauce.

BEAT until smooth. Pack into a 16 ounce crock or jar. Refrigerate at least 6 hours. Serve at room temperature. Makes 2 cups or 12 appetizer servings.

Nutritional Analysis:

	Original	Lowfat Version
Kcals. =	120	61
Chol. =	34 mg	10 mg
Sodium =	154 mg	119 mg
Fat =	11 grams	5 grams
Fat % =	83 %	73 %

SESAME CHEDDAR BALLS

Original Recipe:

1 cup flour
1 cube butter or margarine
1 tsp. dry mustard

2 cups grated cheddar cheese
Sesame seeds

Alterations:

*Half finely ground whole wheat flour
*2 Tbls. diet margarine

* ¼ cup + 2 Tbls. nonfat cream cheese
*Use lowfat cheddar
*2 Tbls. sesame seeds

Directions:

CUT margarine and nonfat cream cheese into flours; add the shredded cheese and form balls. Dip tops of cheese balls into sesame seeds and place seed side up on a non-stick cookie sheet. Bake at 400 for about 10 minutes. Makes about 20 balls.

Nutritional Analysis:

	Original	Lowfat Version
Kcals. =	120	52
Chol. =	12 mg	3 mg
Sodium =	128 mg	51 mg
Fat =	9 grams	2 grams
Fat % =	70 %	37 %

CRACKERJACKS

Original Recipe:

8 cups air-popped popcorn
¾ cup dry roasted peanuts
⅓ cup honey
⅓ cup butter

Alterations:

*Omit peanuts
* ½ cup honey
*2 Tbls. diet margarine
*1 Tbl. peanut butter

Directions:

COMBINE honey, diet margarine, and peanut butter in a small non-stick saucepan. Heat until smooth and bubbly; pour mixture over popcorn and toss thoroughly to coat. Spread onto a non-stick cookie sheet and bake at 325 for about 10-15 minutes (stir once halfway through baking time). 8 (1cup) servings.

Nutritional Analysis:

	Original	Lowfat Version
Kcals. =	217	118
Chol. =	21 mg	0 mg
Sodium =	67 mg	45 mg
Fat =	14 grams	3 grams
Fat % =	58 %	20 %

LIGHT CUSTARD SAUCE

Original Recipe:

½ cup sugar
4 egg yolks
1 tsp. cornstarch
1 ¾ cups milk

1 Tbls. vanilla

Alterations:

* ½ cup Egg Beaters
*1 - 1 ½ Tbls. cornstarch
** ¾ cup skim milk/ 1 cup evaporated
    skim*

Directions:

COMBINE the sugar with the *Egg Beaters* and mix well. Combine the cornstarch and milk and stir over medium heat. Heat until mixture thickens slightly and gradually stir in egg mixture. Continue stirring until hot. Remove from stove and stir in vanilla. Makes 2 cups or 6 servings. Serve over fruit or plain lowfat cake.

Nutritional Analysis:

	Original	Lowfat Version
Kcals. =	148	123
Chol. =	152 mg	2 mg
Sodium =	40 mg	102 mg
Fat =	6 grams	0 grams
Fat % =	35 %	1 %

CUSTARD

PESTO SAUCE

Ingredients:

4 cloves garlic
1 Tbls. pine nuts
1 ½ cups chopped fresh basil
½ cup chopped fresh parsley
⅓ cup grated Parmesan cheese
1 Tbls. olive oil
¾ cup oil-free Italian dressing

Directions:

PROCESS garlic and pine nuts until minced. Add remaining ingredients and process all until smooth. Makes 1 cup or 16 servings.

Nutritional Analysis:

Kcals. =	33
Chol. =	2 mg
Sodium =	52 mg
Fat =	2 grams
Fat % =	60 %

HOLLANDAISE SAUCE

Original Ingredients:

3 egg yolks
1 - 2 Tbls. fresh lemon juice
Pinch of salt
½ lb. sweet butter, melted

White pepper to taste

Alterations:

* ⅜ cup Egg Beaters

*Omit
*1 cup evaporated skim milk +1 Tbls.
cornstarch + 2 Tbls. diet margarine
+ 1 tsp. butter flavoring

Directions:

STIR together the evaporated skim milk, cornstarch, *Egg Beaters*, and butter flavoring. Heat and stir constantly until thickened. Remove from heat and stir in the diet margarine until melted. Add the lemon juice; stir and serve immediately. Make 1 ½ cups or 6 servings.

Nutritional Analysis:

	Original	Lowfat Version
Kcals. =	302	71
Chol. =	189 mg	2 mg
Sodium =	54 mg	149 mg
Fat =	33 grams	2 grams
Fat % =	97 %	25 %

ADAPTED FROM THE SILVER PALATE COOKBOOK

BECHAMEL SAUCE

Original Recipe:
4 Tbls. sweet butter

6 Tbls. flour
Salt, pepper, nutmeg to taste
2 cups milk

Alterations:
*2 Tbls. diet margarine + 1 tsp. butter
*   flavoring*
*2 Tbls. cornstarch
*Omit salt
*2 cups evaporated skim milk

Directions:

COMBINE the milk, cornstarch, seasonings, margarine, and butter flavoring in a non-stick pan. Heat and stir constantly until thickened. Makes 2 cups of sauce or 8 servings.

Nutritional Analysis:	Original	Lowfat Version
Kcals. =	110	68
Chol. =	24 mg	3 mg
Sodium =	66 mg	107 mg
Fat =	8 grams	2 grams
Fat % =	64 %	20 %

ADAPTED FROM THE SILVER PALATE COOKBOOK

TARRAGON WINE SAUCE

Original Recipe:

¾ cup sweet white wine
1 Tbls. finely chopped green onion
½ tsp. dried tarragon
Pinch of salt
3 egg yolks
1 cup sweet butter, melted

Alterations:

*1 tsp. tarragon
*Omit
* ⅜ cup Egg Beaters
*1 skim milk + 2 Tbls. diet margarine +
4 tsp. cornstarch + 1 tsp. butter
flavoring

Directions:

COMBINE the wine, onion, and tarragon in a non-stick saucepan. Bring to a boil and simmer until reduced to a few spoonfuls. In a large measuring cup, mix the egg substitute, skim milk, diet margarine, cornstarch, and butter flavoring. Stir into the wine mixture gradually and cook until thickened. Makes about 1 ½ cups or 6 servings. Serve over fish or poultry.

Nutritional Analysis:	Original	Lowfat Version
Kcals. =	322	73
Chol. =	189 mg	1 mg
Sodium =	56 mg	123 mg
Fat =	33 grams	2 grams
Fat % =	97 %	24 %

ADAPTED FROM THE SILVER PALATE COOKBOOK

FANCY GREEN BEANS

Original Recipe:

2 cans French-style green beans
   (partially drained)

2 cans cream of mushroom soup

¼ cup slivered almonds
½ cup grated cheddar cheese
Bread crumbs

Alterations:

*20 oz. frozen French-cut green beans
   or Oriental Mix (green beans,
   broccoli, mushrooms, onions)
*1 can Healthy Request cream of
   mushroom soup mixed with ½
   can nonfat milk
*1 Tbls. chopped almonds
* ¼ cup shredded lowfat cheddar cheese
*Whole wheat bread crumbs

Directions:

MICROWAVE frozen vegetables (no water added) for 10 minutes on high; or steam until tender. Combine all ingredients and bake at 325 for about 25 minutes. Serves 6 generously.

Nutritional Analysis:

	Original	Lowfat Version
Kcals. =	230	112
Chol. =	11 mg	21 mg
Sodium =	1588 mg	302 mg
Fat =	14 grams	4 grams
Fat % =	54 %	30 %

CORNY SPOON BREAD

Original Recipe:

9 Tbls. butter
16 oz. canned corn, undrained
3 cups milk
1 tsp. salt
1 cup white cornmeal
3 egg yolks
1 Tbls. sugar
¼ tsp. nutmeg
⅛ tsp. cayenne pepper
3 egg whites, beaten until stiff

Alterations:

* ⅓ cup diet margarine
*16 oz. frozen corn + ½ cup apple juice
*3 cups skim milk
*A sprinkle of salt
*1 cup yellow cornmeal
* ⅜ cup Egg Beaters

Directions:

PREHEAT oven to 350. Spray a large casserole dish. Place corn and apple juice in a saucepan. Add 2 cups skim milk and bring to a boil over high heat. Stir in cornmeal slowly to keep smooth and boil until thick. Remove from heat and stir in the diet margarine and remaining 1 cup skim milk. When smooth, add egg substitute, sugar, and spices. Fold in beaten egg whites and turn into the casserole. Bake uncovered for 30 to 35 minutes. Serves 6 - 8.

Nutritional Analysis:

	Original	Lowfat Version
Kcals. =	404	243
Chol. =	170 mg	2 mg
Sodium =	783 mg	476 mg
Fat =	25 grams	6 grams
Fat % =	55 %	21 %

GRANNY'S LITE SAUSAGE STUFFING

Original Recipe:

2 whole onions, chopped
   one red/one yellow
⅓ bunch celery (2 cups)
1 bell pepper, chopped
1 bunch green onions, chopped
1 - 2 cloves minced garlic
⅓ lb. cooked pork sausage
9 oz. packaged stuffing cubes
⅔ can cream chicken soup
1 tsp. salt
½ tsp. pepper
½ cup turkey drippings

Alterations:

* ⅓ lb. cooked ground turkey sausage
*1 ½ packages
*Use Healthy Request
*Omit

* ½ cup low-sodium chicken broth

Directions:

IN A NON-STICK PAN, saute onion until almost soft; add celery, continuing to stir and saute. Add bell pepper, green onions, and garlic; continue to stir while sauteing. Remove from heat, stir in cooked ground turkey (pre-spiced for sausage flavor - see below), pepper, and bread cubes along with the cream of chicken soup. Spread stuffing in a non-stick 9X13 pan (stuffing should be only 1 ½ to 2 inches deep). Just before baking, pour chicken broth or defatted turkey broth over the top. Bake at 350 approximately 30 minutes. Makes 8 servings.

Nutritional Analysis:	Original	Lowfat Version
Kcals. =	372	210
Chol. =	29 mg	14 mg
Sodium =	1152 mg	588 mg
Fat =	23 grams	5 grams
Fat % =	56 %	20 %

NOTE: Combine ⅓ lb. ground turkey with the following spices early in the day and let stand in the refrigerator until cooking time: ½ tsp. anise seed, ½ tsp. thyme, ½ tsp. poultry seasoning, dash of pepper and salt, ⅛ tsp. onion powder.

WALNUT BROCCOLI

Original Recipe:

3 packages frozen broccoli (10 oz. each)
1/4 cup butter
1/2 cup chopped onion
4 Tbls. flour
1 1/2 Tbls. chicken broth (dry)
2 cups milk

6- 8 oz. Pepperidge Farm *stuffing mix*
2/3 cup water
4 Tbls. butter
2/3 cup chopped walnuts

Alterations:

*1 Tbls. diet margarine

*2 Tbls. cornstarch
*Use low-sodium brand
*1 cup skim milk + 1 cup evaporated
    skim milk

*2 Tbls. diet margarine
* 1/3 cup chopped walnuts

Directions:

MICROWAVE the packages of chopped frozen broccoli until just tender; drain. Spray a casserole dish and cover bottom of dish with cooked broccoli. Combine melted margarine, onion, and dry chicken broth mix in a non-stick sauce pan; saute onion until tender. Mix cornstarch with the 2 cups of milk and add slowly to the broth/onion mixture. Cook and stir until smooth and thickened. Pour milk mixture over broccoli. Combine the stuffing mix with the water and melted margarine; add walnuts and put over top of broccoli. Bake at 400 for 20 minutes. Do not cover. 8 servings.

Nutritional Analysis:

	Original	Lowfat Version
Kcals. =	332	211
Chol. =	41 mg	3 mg
Sodium =	519 mg	496 mg
Fat =	21 grams	7 grams
Fat % =	55 %	27 %

PINEAPPLE DRESSING

Original Recipe:

½ cup soft butter or margarine

½ cup sugar
4 eggs

16 oz. crushed pineapple, undrained
6 slices of firm white bread, cubed

Alterations:

* *¼ cup diet margarine + ¼ cup*
 nonfat cream cheese
* *¼ - ⅓ cup sugar*
**1 cup* Egg Beaters *(or ½ cup* Egg
 Beaters *+ 4 egg whites)*

**Use cracked wheat or whole wheat
 bread*

Directions:

CREAM the diet margarine, nonfat cream cheese, and sugar. Add the egg substitute and stir in the pineapple. Fold in the bread cubes, pour into a non-stick or sprayed 1 ½ quart casserole dish, and bake for 45 minutes at 350 until top is browned. Serve with a slice of baked lean turkey ham or baked breast of chicken and vegetables, of course. Makes 4 - 6 side dish servings.

Nutritional Analysis:

	Original	Lowfat Version
Kcals. =	370	245
Chol. =	183 mg	0 mg
Sodium =	315 mg	317 mg
Fat =	20 grams	5 grams
Fat % =	47 %	18 %

PINEAPPLE ACORN
SQUASH

Ingredients:

1 baked acorn squash
4 Tbls. crushed pineapple and juice
2 Tbls. brown sugar
Sprinkle of Molly McButter
Dash of nutmeg and cinnamon

Directions:

MIX cooked squash with remaining ingredients and warm in the microwave for about 2 or 3 minutes on high. Serves 4.

Nutritional Analysis:

Kcals. =	99
Chol. =	0 mg
Sodium =	9 mg
Fat =	0 grams
Fat % =	1 %

Notes